**REFIG**

*Jürgen Habermas and the Possibilities of Political Change*

J. Craig Hanks

University Press of America,® Inc.
Lanham · New York · Oxford

Copyright © 2002 by
University Press of America,® Inc.
4720 Boston Way
Lanham, Maryland 20706
UPA Acquisitions Department (301) 459-3366

PO Box 317
Oxford
OX2 9RU, UK

All rights reserved
Printed in the United States of America
British Library Cataloging in Publication Information Available

**Library of Congress Cataloging-in-Publication Data**

Hanks, J. Craig (James Craig)
Refiguring critical theory : Jürgen Habermas and the possibilities
of political change / J. Craig Hanks.
p. cm
Includes bibliographical references and index.
1. Critical theory. 2. Reason. 3. Habermas, Jürgen.
4. Democracy—Philosophy. I. Title.

B809.3 . H364 2002
193—dc21      2002026731 CIP

ISBN 0-7618-2363-8 (clothbound : alk. ppr.)
ISBN 0-7618-2364-6 (paperback : alk. ppr.)

∞™ The paper used in this publication meets the minimum
requirements of American National Standard for Information
Sciences—Permanence of Paper for Printed Library Materials,
ANSI Z39.48—1984

Dedicated to my parents,
Alan and Beverly Hanks

# Contents

| | |
|---|---|
| Preface | vii |
| Acknowledgments | xi |
| Chapter I: The Origins of The Theory of Inner Colonization | 1 |
| Chapter II: The Frankfurt School: The Critique of Instrumental Rationality | 31 |
| Chapter III: Habermas' Initial Reformulation of Critical Theory | 55 |
| Chapter IV: The Colonization of The Lifeworld | 77 |
| Chapter V: Towards A Critical Theory of Habermas | 91 |
| Chapter VI: Thinking the Totality: Habermas and Post-Structuralism | 109 |
| Chapter VII: Some Concluding Thoughts: Salvaging Critical Theory, Or The Necessity of Coalitions | 115 |
| Notes | 121 |
| Bibliography | 161 |
| Index | 173 |
| About the Author | 175 |

# Preface

I write these words on the six-month anniversary of the events of September 11, 2001. There has been, in the intervening months, much talk about how things have fundamentally changed in the United States. Supposedly we have all slowed down, cleared our heads of superficial concerns, and now have clear individual and societal commitments to peace and democracy. Supposedly. Or, perhaps we have again committed the United States to playing cop of the world, once again defining the world in clear terms of "us versus them" – not unlike the way we understood the world when the precursors of the Taliban regime were our friends the "Afghan freedom fighters" in the war against global communism.

Into this context I offer some thoughts on the nature of democracy. I understand democracy as a radical project of self-determination, one not fully realized. In this sense, democracy is a regulative ideal, something we aim for, the exact nature of which is always receding ahead of us. The current U.S. led war raises important questions, both in the United States and around the world, about self-determination and about the nature of democracy.

The setting of this work is not only the current "war on terrorism," but also the ongoing intellectual debates about postmodernism. What is/was it? Is/was it here, or in the future? Is/was it fundamentally different from modernism, or a continuation of certain tendencies within modernity? Is/was it desirable, avoidable, the end of history, the fall of Western civilization, the celebration of diversity, or the end of any possible value distinctions? Is postmodernity the end of the subject? And, if so, what does this mean for political and moral agency? Or, is/was postmodernity one or more of these? Or, none of the above? Admittedly this debate has been fun for some members of the academy, meaningless to others, and of great political and intellectual importance to still others. One central issue in the debate is how we understand who has a say, about who has a voice in the decisions that shape individual lives and the direction of societies. In other words, the debate about postmodernism is, at least in part, a debate about the nature of democracy.

Although the debaters will argue that the debate is about the state (or direction) of culture as a whole, it isn't clear that the culture as a whole, Western Culture that is, has engaged in this debate. At least, it isn't clear that most people have spent much time over food or drink debating i) whether or not we live in postmodernity or ii) the virtues and failings of postmodern theory. Nonetheless, as this debate has unfolded, the world has seen many events which intellectuals from all portions of the political spectrum have interpreted as evidence of some fact about postmodernity. The fall of totalitarian regimes in the Soviet Union and Eastern and Central Europe was hailed as evidence of the end of history, as the end, or the triumph, of modernity. We are, either happily or lamentably depending on one's view of the present age, at a point when big ideas, metatheories, or ideologies can no longer have a hold on masses of people and "move" history. More recently we have witnessed the splintering of community in Eastern and Central Europe; resurgent nationalism; an increase in racially motivated identity politics, war and hate crimes (think of the treatment of Turkish "guest workers" in Germany, or Bosnia, or Prop 187 in California in the 1994 elections); and a push to restrict the civil liberties of "foreigners" and those who refuse to be well-normed -- who refuse to fit in (in the United States these efforts include: laws against loitering, attempts to outlaw homelessness, the war on drugs, a crackdown on speech in the electronic community, and so on).

The debates about the meaning of recent local and global changes are ongoing both in and out of the academy, in and out of official politics and lived in our daily lives. I do not claim that I settle these debates. I do think that thinking carefully about both theoretical and practical questions and solutions is necessary in days like these, and I aim to make some small contribution to such thinking. I do not dwell long with postmodernism in what follows, at least not explicitly. But, questions about the newness of our situation, and about the difference of the present from the recent and distant past are at work throughout. So to is a concern to trace the trajectory of one line of thinking about self-determination and the many ways in which we humans systematically restrict it.

In this work I propose that a certain tradition of thinking about the relations between i) what we do and who we are (being); ii) what and how we think (consciousness); and iii) who and what we might become is useful in thinking and acting in the present situation. I refer to the tradition known as Critical Theory that has roots in left-Hegelianism, and especially the work of Marx. This tradition has been explicitly concerned with presenting an analysis of the social world with practical intent.

One of the most important thinkers working in this tradition today is Jürgen Habermas. His work offers us a way to think about political possibilities and subjectivity which offers a way between a cynical postmodern throwing up of our hands and a neo-conservative reaction against the gains of modernity and the liberalization of culture (this reaction is itself highly cynical). The case I make is that our analysis of his work will be incomplete if we do not understand it as growing out of a tradition of radical political thinking. I argue that understanding his work as coming out of this tradition (from Hegel through Marx and the early Critical Theorists) will contextualize and enrich our understanding of his critique and contribution to contemporary theory and thus contextualize and enrich its importance to us.

In this work I trace theories of the relationship between being and consciousness from Marx through Lukacs and the Frankfurt School to Habermas' recent work *The Theory of Communicative Action*. I argue that in terms of his stated goal of providing a critical social theory with practical intent Habermas has been only partially successful. I present an account of Habermas' theory and claim it is potentially more politically efficacious than post-structuralist theories, though only if his theory is attentive to the concerns of those same post-structuralist theories. I argue that at a certain level of abstraction Habermas is right in his account of our present situation. I also argue that he falls short of his goal in so far as his theory fails to take adequate account of i) many actually existing struggles for political self-determination, and ii) many hypotheses for alternative social organization that do not agree with his assumptions about validity and consensus.

# Acknowledgements

As with most any book, this one is really the product of many people, and those who deserve thanks are numerous. Thanks are due to friends, mentors, and colleagues who have encouraged my work and whose words have helped shaped this book. Some have read, listened to, and commented on portions of this book. All have provided intellectual and emotional criticism and encouragement. They include: Larry Hickman, Rick Roderick, Stacey Haire, John McDermott, Erin McKenna, George Trey, Bill Martin, Martin Beck Matustik, Patricia Huntington, Emily Pantazi, Rolf Goebel, Stephen Waring, Tamsin Lorraine, Alison Brown, Amanda Gould, and Leslie MacAvoy.

The research for this work was partially funded by the University of Alabama in Huntsville Humanities Center and the National Endowment for the Humanities, which provided a summer research grant. Kara Sweeney provided careful, patient, and thoughtful assistance during the term of the grant. She, and the many other students with whom I have had the privilege of reading works dealt with in this essay; deserve boundless thanks for what they have taught me. From Brian Martine, Andy Cling and Bill Wilkerson, my departmental colleagues at UAH, I learned much, and their personal and intellectual support have been invaluable.

Special thanks are due María Inmaculada de Melo-Martín, whose intellectual energy, passion for justice, philosophical acumen, and joyful living provide constant inspiration, and a daily reminder of why I practice philosophy. Without her kind support this book would not have seen the light of day.

# CHAPTER I

# THE ORIGINS OF THE THEORY OF INNER COLONIZATION

### Setting the Stage: Commodity Fetishism and the "Crisis of Marxism"

It is not the consciousness of men that determines their being, but, on the contrary, their social being that determines their consciousness.[1]

This brief enigmatic passage from Karl Marx's *Preface to a Critique of Political Economy* expresses one of the central claims of Marx's work. A cursory reading tells us that Marx is claiming that the shape of human consciousness and its products (art, religion, law, philosophy...) at any given time and place is dependent upon the social relations in which we humans find ourselves. If we find ourselves in social relations that limit the range of social action, then the reach of our consciousness will also be limited. Determining the nature of this relationship has been one of the primary concerns of philosophers in the Marxist tradition. This is so, in part, because Marxist philosophers have been concerned to articulate the possibilities and reasons for radical social transformation. On what ground can legitimate demands for social change be based? What segment of society is likely to articulate a demand for justice and become an origin of a movement for social change?

Within the Marxist tradition what is known as Western Marxism[2] has had a special interest in the shapes which consciousness has taken under subsequent and increasingly complex social formations. In this essay, I will examine some recent attempts by Jürgen Habermas, working within the Critical Theory[3] version of Western Marxism, to address these issues. I will be developing a reading of Habermas through a Marxist tradition. In order to do so I will spend some time setting the intellectual stage on which Marx's work took place. That is, I will trace some of the Hegelian and Kantian roots of Marxism.

When Marx addresses the question of social consciousness and social being, he is especially interested in the forms they take in his world of the 19th century. This was the era of the first wave of rapid growth of industrial capitalism in Europe and North America. Marx's was a world in which factory labor for the production of commodities was coming to be **the** form of social activity for ever larger numbers of people. In Volume I, Chapter 1, Section IV of *Capital*, Marx describes what he calls the fetishism of commodities. As he explains, under capitalism all social relations are mediated by the commodity form.

> The mysterious character of the commodity-form consists therefore simply in the fact that the commodity reflects the social characteristics of man's own labour as objective characteristics of the products of labour themselves, as the socio-natural properties of these things. Hence it also reflects the social relation of the producers to the sum total of labour as a social relation between objects, a relation which exists apart from and outside the producers . . .. It is nothing but the definite social relation between men themselves which assumes here, for them the fantastic form of a relation between things.[4]

Marx is arguing that under capitalism all social relations appear as relations between commodities. That is, all relations between persons appear as relations between things.

As Marx observes, a commodity is the embodiment of human labor, and the value of a commodity expresses the socially necessary labor time required for its production. Commodities can only be exchanged if they can be considered equivalent in some respect. As noted, all commodities are products of human labor, and it is this origin that all commodities have in common. Human labor is not all the same, so in order for different types of human labor to be considered as equivalent all labor is translated into its equivalent quantity of simple human labor. Under capitalism, qualitatively different forms of human labor are considered in the abstract as universal, or simple labor. Marx explains: "A commodity may be the outcome of the most complicated labour, but through its **value** it is posited as equal to the product of simple labor, hence it represents only a specific quantity of simple labor."[5] This process goes on all the time; it allows the exchange of qualitatively different labor and commodities. Money, as the universal equivalent, functions to mediate the commodity exchange relation (including the exchange of human labor-time for wages).

All of this, especially the introduction of money as the universal equivalent not only "goes on behind the back of the producers,"[6] but is also beyond the analysis of traditional political economy.[7] For the economist, Marx argues, value is understood not as abstract human labor, but as an aspect of the object itself.

According to Marx, the nature of social relations under capitalism is to appear as relations between things (or objects) and not as relations between people (or subjects). This appearance is not an illusion, but the actuality of lived experience under capitalism. It is these fetishized relationships that constitute our being.[8] Marx claimed that under capitalist relations of production human beings will be constructed so as to relate to each other in the same ways they relate to any other commodity. Under capitalism, we relate to each other as things. The social character of production is occluded because every person seems to be pursuing her or his own interest. The only consciously social relationship, in capitalism, is the exchange relation. And even in exchange relations, humans trade labor and commodities without being aware of the social relations embodied therein.

The labor of individuals is an element of the total labor of society. But, it appears as such only when the products of labor enter into exchange relations. In this situation (i.e.: in capitalism), the relations between individual workers are not understood as "direct social relations between persons in their work, but rather as material relations between persons and social relations between things."[9]

The discovery "that the products of labour, in so far as they are values are merely the material expressions of the human labour expended to produce them"[10] does not destroy the semblance of objectivity to the claim that different kinds of human labor can be reduced to "human labor in the abstract." This truth about commodities, that qualitatively different forms of human labor will be equated as abstract human labor, is only a truth for this historically specific form of production. Nonetheless, the claim that value exists in the objects, "appears to those caught up in the relations of commodity production to be just as ultimately valid as the fact that the scientific dissection of the air into its component parts left the atmosphere itself unadulterated in its physical configuration."[11] What has happened is that value has been ascribed as a natural attribute of commodities that is only realized in the social relation of exchange. The fact of the production of material objects by human labor in a social system where the processes of production and exchange have priority over human needs is accepted as "a self-evident and nature imposed necessity."[12]

Consciousness is, on this account, but a reflection of fetishized social relationships. As such, consciousness will be historically variable. Since the social relations of human beings are historically contingent, social being is itself dynamic. With the ascendance of the commodity form (i.e.: with the rise and spread of capitalism), all aspects of being have become fetishized.

To understand exactly what it means for social relations to appear as relations between commodities, we need to make a closer examination of the commodity form itself. Commodities are the product of human labor, but not every product of human labor is a commodity. Marx explains:

> A thing can be useful, and a product of human labour, without becoming a commodity. He who satisfies his own need with the product of his own labour admittedly creates use-values, but not commodities. In order to produce the latter, he must not only produce use-values, but use-values for others, social use-values. (And not merely for others . . . . In order to become a commodity, the product must be transferred to another person . . . through the medium of exchange.)[13]

The conditions for the commodity-form first arise when and only when the products of human labor are produced for exchange, that is, when they are produced for sale in the marketplace.

Since our being is determined by our position in the commodity relations of capitalism, (when human labor is just another commodity on the market) our consciousness becomes commodity consciousness. Commodities have no self-determination, being not subjects but objects. They cannot grasp history and direct it toward their liberation. Commodities, as objects, cannot act and are not worthy of moral respect. Commodity consciousness is self-conception as commodity.

All inside commodity relations (or, all who occupy some position in capitalist relations of production) will conceive of themselves as commodities. As such, self-understanding will not include the idea of self-determination, or will conceive of self-determination as always already bounded by existing social structures (which may appear as natural, and not social). Self-determination will take place within the strictures of the market, and thus is "economic man" born. Commodity consciousness is unable to conceive of the conscious human direction of history toward human liberation in part because commodities are discrete, independent, disconnected objects. As such, commodities are separable, have nothing in common with each other, and can only pursue their own self-interest.

Marx uses this model of the relation between being and consciousness to fuel his critique of capitalism. In constructing this critique, he uses the language of classical political economy. [14] He does so in order to show how, in its own terms, capitalism will breakdown/self-destruct. Furthermore, if he is correct that social being determines consciousness and that language is a manifestation of consciousness, then there is no other language he could speak.

The use of economic language limits his analysis and critique. In using the language of classical political economy to critique capitalism, Marx seems to accept a fetishized concept of social being which reduces all needs to economic needs and the whole of being to the worker's place (or the owner's, or the manager's, or the intellectual's place) in commodity relations.[15]

Marx's model of the relation between being and consciousness limits his critique in other ways. For instance, in *Capital* Marx's project is to provide an account of capitalism and its inner dynamics, capitalism's objective tendencies toward crisis and the possibilities of its breakdown and replacement with socialism. By speaking the language of commodities, Marx is limited in his ability to articulate socialist alternatives to capitalism. Not only is the alternative difficult, if not impossible, to articulate, but so too are the time, place, and method of bringing about a socialist alternative. Because of the language he uses, and because of the economic determinist nature of his model of society, Marx must claim not only that a capitalist crisis is a necessary condition for radical social change, but he must also claim that a crisis in capitalism **will** lead to radical social change.[16]

The traces of Hegel are evident in this portion of Marx's work. For Hegel, history is the story of the dialectical progression of freedom moved forward by reason. He summarizes this claim near the end of *The Philosophy of History*, "the History of the World is nothing but the development of the Idea of Freedom."[17] Hegel argues that in spite of the seeming unreasonableness and pointless suffering in history we can give an account of history as a reasonable process.

According to Hegel, each moment in history contains certain possibilities and limitations, certain ideals are held forth as the ideals of society and for some reason, which will vary according to the circumstances, society falls short of is own ideals. The claim here is that every society articulates goals and ideals to which it (its people) aspire. Freedom, in a society, is the freedom to achieve the ideals of that society. So long as there are obstacles between people and the realization of the aims and goals of their historically specific society, then they are not free - on their own terms. On this account no unfree situation can be rational because every person seeks freedom as something good for him or herself. For this reason, once the claims of freedom are presented, they cannot be denied and the existing unfree state of affairs will deserve to perish. The actual operation of human reason can point out the deficiencies of actually existing social systems, and the historically observed human struggle for freedom, which is not just an idea, but a passion, will move history and construct new social forms. This is how the dialectic of history moves, in fits and starts and often skipping from one geographic location to another, each moment containing the possibilities of its own dissolution and overcoming.

Thus, every period in history is but a partial realization of its own ideals and will be overcome as humans attempt to realize those ideals. As history progresses, it does so by building on that which came before. Thus, the best, most true, and most free features of previous societies will be refigured in the construction of the new. The ultimate goal of history is the realization of the final stage of freedom.[18] Hegel often writes as if this final stage has been achieved in his time.[19]

Marx adopts Hegel's account of history as the dialectical unfolding of successive stages. In *The German Ideology*, Marx argues that history moves as a result of the dialectical relationship between forces and relations of production. Every historical stage has certain productive capacities. These are determined by the technological capacities and the organization of production. As technological advances occur, they are constrained by existing relations of production. That is, the full potential of new technologies cannot be realized until the relations of production (in *The German Ideology*, "forms of intercourse") are burst asunder and the contradiction between new productive capacity and the existing organization of production is resolved in a new, and 'higher,' historical stage.[20] Marx summarizes in his 1859 Preface to *A Critique of Political Economy:*

> At a certain stage of their development, the material productive forces of society come in conflict with the existing relations of production, or -- what is but a legal expression of the same thing -- with property relations within which they have been at work hitherto. From forms of development of the productive forces these relations turn into their fetters. Then begins an epoch of social revolution.[21]

Marx follows Hegel's account of history and argues that each historical stage generates the principles of its own dissolution, and that each successive stage is "the result of the activity of a whole succession of generations, each standing on the shoulders of the preceding one."[22] In Marx's description of history, just as in Hegel's, each stage grows of necessity out of the previous stage. However, for Marx, history is not the story of a world that is the immediate appearance of Mind. Rather, the ideas, or conscious self-descriptions of every age are reflections of material conditions, and material conditions progress following the dialectic of history,[23] a dialectic that unfolds according to the constant human opposition to historically specific forms of oppression. Or, as Marx and Engels wrote in *The Communist Manifesto*, "The history of all hitherto existing society is the history of class struggle."[24]

Using this model of the determination of consciousness by historically necessary successive modes of production, Marx has given us a providential fable. The progression from mode of production to mode of production, from form of consciousness to form of consciousness will continue until revolution and the withering away of the state. On this account, socialism becomes an inevitable product of the necessary progression of human history.

By his own account, Marx would say that his thought was conditioned by his historical situation. He was unable to grasp the possibility that capitalism might be flexible enough to right itself after every crisis. His tale, with its expectation of an inevitable revolution, functions as a strategy of containment,[25] containment of the terror of a self-correcting capitalism. By treating social progress as inevitable he suppresses the nightmare of history: the possibility that oppressive economic and social organizations might find ways to perpetuate themselves into all possible futures.

In addition, this model seems to no longer justify in our time much, if any, confidence in a socialist future. On certain accounts of how we ought to evaluate theories,[26] Marx's theory has been falsified by the failure of democratic attempts to peacefully turn European states to socialism, the failure of revolutions in Europe after the First World War and by the failure of attempts to create liberated and liberating socialist societies in the Soviet Union and Eastern Europe and China. Thus we arrive at the so-called "crisis of Marxism".[27]

Or so the story goes.[28]

One way to overcome this crisis might be to reexamine the nature of the relation between being and consciousness. If it is possible that the relation is not one of strict determination but of reciprocal interaction, then consciousness might be constructed as relatively autonomous.[29] If this is the case, or if this is conceivably the case, then any attempt to reconstruct Marx's account of life under capitalism will need to include an account of the nature and role of consciousness. Furthermore, if one is to attempt to reconstruct Marx's account in a way which will serve as a map for social change and explain the fact that radical social transformation along socialist lines has not occurred under conditions of advanced capitalism, then one will need an account of the subjective conditions necessary for radical social change and the ways in which the realization of these subjective conditions is thwarted. That is, one will need an account of, what Jürgen Habermas calls the "colonization of the lifeworld" (or, the colonization of everyday life) in all its dimensions, including the colonization of consciousness. In other words, any attempt to reconstruct Marx's project in such a way as to account for socialism's lack of success must include an account of capitalism as the colonization of subjectivity.

Jürgen Habermas has attempted just such a project. His attempt requires going "beyond" the paradigm of production that is central to Marx's account. Habermas introduces another sphere of action and rationality, the sphere of communicative action.

In order to evaluate Habermas' work, it is necessary to trace out his historical and intellectual antecedents. Such a task requires beginning with an examination of Marx's account of the alienation of labor in *The Economic and Philosophic Manuscripts of 1844*. Having thus begun, I will follow the development of the theory of the colonization of subjectivity from Marx through Lukacs' theory of reification to the

Frankfurt School critique of instrumental reason and one-dimensional society.

After setting the stage in this way, I will be ready to consider Habermas' account of the colonization of the lifeworld. First, I will analyze his early work. This will involve examining his theory of systematically distorted communication, and his account of the ideal speech situation.

I will then turn to Habermas' more recent work. Drawing on the work of Parsons, Mead and Husserl he distinguishes between lifeworld and social system. Making use of the theory of systematically distorted communication and drawing on Marxist/Frankfurt school theories of the colonization of social consciousness, Habermas discusses the fate of subjectivity and the probable locations of social crisis under conditions of late capitalism.[30]

Finally, to evaluate Habermas, and to determine if his theory is not also functioning as a strategy of containment (and is in that sense an 'ideology'[31]), we will examine some accounts of our present situation, a situation that might be called "nightmare capitalism". We will evaluate Habermas according to his own self-proclaimed goal of constructing a critical social theory with practical intent.

## From Hegel and Feuerbach to Marx: Theories of Alienation

Marx's account of alienation first appears in detail in his *Economic and Philosophic Manuscripts of 1844*. In this account we find three primary intellectual traditions converging in Marx's work: German idealism, British political economy, and French socialism.[32] Marx draws the notion of humans as self-creative from the tradition of German idealism. He transforms this notion into the claims i) that human alienation can only be overcome in practice that is aimed at self-control of productive (creative) activities and ii) that creating the space for this sort of practice requires collective activity.

The claim that human beings are self-dependent, autonomous and rational beings receives what is one of its most compelling formulations in the work of Immanuel Kant. Kant argues that the very nature of humans as self-dependent rational beings demands freedom. It is only if people are able to freely exercise their reason that they can realize their potential as rational beings.[33] It should be noted that this account of freedom rests upon a transcendental argument in which human reason (the subject of knowledge or, in this case, the subject of freedom) posits freedom as a function of the intelligible world of things-in-themselves (the object world), a world of which we can have no knowledge.[34] Thus, though freedom is posited by humans, it is something that humans can never fully realize.[35]

Not willing to accept Kant's world of unknowable things-in-themselves, Hegel conceives of human self-creation as a process, a process that reveals the progress of human freedom and reveals freedom to be "not something which they have, as humans, but which they are."[36] But, the story of this process is not just the story of human self-creation, it is the story of Being (God), Being's necessary self-alienation, and the realization of the fullness of Being in Becoming (history).[37] Pure Being, in its attempt to think itself (to achieve self-consciousness) thinks Nothingness. Hegel writes, "But this mere Being, as it is mere abstraction, is therefore the absolute negative: which, in a similarly immediate aspect is just **Nothing**."[38]

Hegel identifies the process of Being externalizing itself in its attempt at self-realization as Becoming. Hegel proceeds to identify determinate being (concrete being in this world) with Becoming.[39] Since Becoming is the actuality of Being's creation of/unity with that which it is not (not-Being or Nothingness), then Becoming is the concrete manifestation of Being's self-alienation. Thus, the fundamental nature of existence (until such time as Being can be fully realized, i.e.: the uniting of subject and object at the end of history) is to be alienated. Marx observes:

> Hegel grasps man's self-estrangement, the alienation of man's essence, man's loss of objectivity and his loss of realness as self-discovery, change of his nature, objectification and realization. In short, within the sphere of abstraction, Hegel conceives of labour as man's act of **self-genesis**--conceives man's relation of himself as an alien being and the manifestation of himself as an alien being to be the emergence of **species consciousness** and **species life**.[40]

Self-consciousness is not possible in isolation, nor is it possible in the initial unity of Being. Self-consciousness is only possible through the creation of that which is other. In order for Being to become self-conscious, it must externalize itself, engage in self-estrangement - the creation of the world. As I mentioned earlier, the full realization of Being occurs through Becoming. That is, Being (or, God) becomes self-conscious through the creation of that which is other (the world), and its development (history). The history of the world is Being becoming self-conscious.

We should take note of the fact that this self-consciousness is only possible through confronting another. Early in *The Phenomenology of Spirit* Hegel discusses what happens when two consciousnesses meet. The dialectic of Lordship and Bondage (or Master and Slave) is especially important for both Hegel and Marx. It is important for Hegel because humans are Being's self-consciousness, thus the overcoming of human estrangement is necessary to overcoming the self-estrangement of Being (or God). For Marx, the importance lies in the possibilities for resistance to oppression which Hegel identifies, Marx is interested not in Being's self-consciousness, but in overcoming human alienation.

Section B, IV, A of the *Phenomenology* is titled "Independence and Dependence of Self-Consciousness: Lordship and Bondage."[41] In this section Hegel describes a two-part dialectic whereby self-consciousness i) struggles with 'the other' for recognition of its own independence, and ii) discovers the dependence of the victor (master or lord) on the vanquished (slave).

Hegel begins by describing the initial contact of two self-consciousnesses. Each needs recognition by the other while simultaneously needing to negate the other's otherness.[42] What ensues is a struggle for dominance in the form of a fight to the death. This struggle has two goals. The first goal is to negate the other (this can take the form of symbolic death, for instance not inviting a rival to your next cookout or cocktail party). In the Master/Slave, this goal is achieved primarily in the dependency of the other. The second goal is to gain conscious affirmation of one's self. Here the notion found in Sartre and Camus that confrontation with death is necessarily the first and most important question of philosophy is helpful in understanding what Hegel means.

In *The Myth of Sisyphus*, Camus writes, "There is but one truly serious philosophical problem, and that is suicide. Judging whether life is or is not worth living amounts to answering the fundamental question of philosophy."[43] Camus, like Hegel, is putting forth the claim that only in a confrontation with the termination of my own existence do I gain confirmation of my self. If I die, then I gain self-certainty. Hegel wrote, "The individual who has not risked his life may well be recognized as a person, but he has not attained to the truth of this recognition as an independent self-consciousness."[44] Only through a confrontation with death can we come to value our own life. The goal of the life and death struggle with the other is as much to affirm my own independent existence, as it is to negate the other.

But, what if I do not die? If I die, then clearly I have risked my life. If I do not, then I need the other as a witness to the struggle. In this way, "[t]his trial by death . . . does away with the truth which was supposed to issue from it."[45] This is so because self-consciousness now depends upon the recognition of the other. A completely autonomous independent self-consciousness is impossible. What I need to affirm and confirm my existence is recognition by another who is my equal -- I need recognition freely given. This is not the result of the dialectic between master and slave. The victor in the struggle becomes the master; the loser becomes the slave. In the second part of the account Hegel argues that neither master nor slave has attained that which each desired -- confirmation of self as a whole and independent being.

In the second part of the Master/Slave dialectic, the master becomes dependent on the slave. Marx found in this inversion a way of understanding the eventual necessity of a working class revolution.

In *The Spirit of Hegel*, Robert Solomon argues that Hegel's account of desire[46] is a necessary component of the Master/Slave story. Solomon writes, "Perhaps the modern word which best fits the master is "jaded," since the fruits of life come to him effortlessly, with instant satisfaction, which leads him therefore to a continuous search for new satisfactions and more extravagant desires."[47] The secret of desire, what we might call the rule of desire, is this: desire does not wish to be satisfied for each satisfaction is only temporary. Desire wishes to be prolonged. In the constant search for new satisfactions the master will grow weak, lazy and dependent.

On the other side of the relationship, the slave is engaging in labor. Hegel had read Adam Smith and followed his valorization of work as self-realization and the source of all value. This means that the master is not only a slave to his or her passions, but is also alienated from the material things that sustain his or her life. The slave enjoys the satisfaction of work and is integrated with the production process. But, at the same time, the product ultimately belongs to the master and the slave is alienated from the product of labor.

For Hegel, all of this is of secondary importance to the question of recognition. The material relations between master and slave are symbolic of the struggle for self-recognition. For Marx, the material relations are constitutive of the struggle for recognition.

Hegel's primary concern is how the master and slave regard each other. Initially the master regards the slave and the slave's labor as existing for the sake of the master. But, this relationship is "one-sided and unequal,"[48] and the master comes to view him or her self as dependent on the slave. The master's recognition of his or her status as master requires the existence of the slave. Thus, even in victory, the master is dependent upon the slave for confirmation of his or her independent existence. Not only is this dependent confirmation of independence contrary to the goals of the struggle, but the nature of the slave's recognition of the master is problematic. The slave's independence has been negated and "what the bondsman does is really the action of the lord."[49] The master cannot receive the kind of recognition s/he desires. S/he cannot receive the recognition of a free and equal being.

The slave understands that s/he is relatively independent of the master. This is accomplished through i) working, ii) understanding the master's dependence, and iii) understanding that s/he can bring about his or her own death and thus attain freedom from the master. Except for working, the slave's independence is only relative because it is defined in relation to the master. And, even in work, the product of labor belongs to the master.

In this situation, neither master nor slave has attained that which was sought in the initial struggle. For this reason, each makes continued, and increasingly desperate efforts to maintain self-consciousness, to become independent, to realize "the whole of objective being."[50]

But, confrontation with another (the object) is actually a confrontation with the self (the subject). Thus, it appears that estrangement is a necessary attribute of self-consciousness. Hegel explains near the end of *The Phenomenology of Spirit*,

> Not until consciousness has given up hope of overcoming that alienation in an external. i.e. alien, manner does it turn to its own present world and discover it as its property, thus taking the first step towards coming down out of the **intellectual world**, or rather towards quickening the abstract element of that world with the actual Self.[51]

Hegel argues that alienation can only be overcome when it is understood as self-alienation, when the subject grasps the object as itself. For Spirit, this means that "until Spirit has completed itself in itself, until it has completed itself as world-Spirit, it cannot reach its consummation as self-conscious Spirit."[52] On the way to final self-consciousness Spirit externalizes itself and then follows the dialectical progression of history until a new unity is achieved.

Being, it turns out, is of necessity alienated in this world (otherwise this world would not be). Thus, human beings, as the self-consciousness of Being, will be alienated. As noted above, Marx understood that on Hegel's account human alienation is but one aspect of the self-alienation of Being. Marx shares with Hegel the claim that estrangement is a necessary moment on the road to a new situation full of the content of history and not the empty initial unity of Hegel's Being. Where they differ is about the subject[s] of history - for Hegel it is Being as such, for Marx the subjects of history are human beings.[53]

Ludwig Feuerbach takes Hegel to task for this abstract idealist account of alienation. He characterizes Hegel as a "realist,"

> A realist in the abstraction from all reality. He negates thought, namely abstract thought; but the negation is itself abstract thought so that the negation of abstraction is itself an abstraction. According to Hegel, philosophy has for an object only "that which is"; but this "is" is itself only an abstracted and ideated "is." Hegel is a thinker who surpasses himself in thought; he wants to grasp the thing itself, but in the thought of the thing.[54]

Feuerbach's point here is similar to that of Marx, Hegel wishes to overcome alienation, to "grasp the thing itself" and yet though he recognizes the role of history on this process, Hegel only reaches for "the thought of the thing." However, if certain things, such as freedom, are more than just thought, or if their realization requires more than just thinking about them, then Hegel is bound to fail in his attempt to reach the thing itself.

Feuerbach takes the account of alienation on a materialist turn. He no longer locates the source of alienation in Being (God), but in human beings. What happens is that human beings take certain aspects of their nature and project them to perfection. This projection takes the shape of God in religion[55] and Being in philosophy.[56] Whereas Hegel believed that thought preceded existence and that human history was the story of Being's (God's) self-alienation, Feuerbach argued that existence and acting in the world proceeded thinking about the world, and that God existed only insofar as humans were divided against each other and alienated from themselves. So, whereas on Hegel's account we are evidence of God's self-alienation, on Feuerbach's account God is evidence of our alienation.

In this materialist inversion of Hegel, Marx believes Feuerbach to be essentially correct. However, Feuerbach has stopped short of what he had hoped to achieve.

> Feuerbach wants sensuous objects, really distinct from the thought objects, but he does not conceive human activity itself as objective activity. Hence in *Das Wesen des Christentums*, he regards the theoretical attitude as the only genuine human attitude.[57]

Feuerbach has recognized the material human source of alienation, but he idealizes it into a critique of religion and philosophy. In doing so, he renders alienation independent of any particular human situation, theorizing it as a transhistorical fact about human existence. Marx wrote, "Feuerbach resolves the religious essence into to human essence. But the human essence is no abstraction inherent in each single individual. In its reality it is the ensemble of social relations."[58]

In his critique of Hegel, Feuerbach has substituted one essence (human) for another (Absolute Being). In so doing, Feuerbach fails to realize the specific sources of alienation found in a particular historical situation. Because of this, Marx explains, "he does not grasp the significance of 'revolutionary', of 'practical-critical' activity."[59] That is, though he recognizes the source of alienation in human beings, Feuerbach claims it is an essential characteristic of human life; therefore, he does not address the specific nature of alienation found in his time nor does he offer any concrete hope of overcoming alienation.

Marx takes up the question of why humans confront the world as alien to them and hostile to their interests in the *Economic and Philosophic Manuscripts of 1844*. Hegel had argued that the subject-object relation (a necessary condition of self-consciousness until the end of history) was necessarily one of alienation, specifically Being's self-alienation. Feuerbach had argued that alienation was a function of a necessary fact about human beings regardless of their historical location. Marx follows Feuerbach in the critique of Hegel, but goes further to argue that the source of the particular form of alienation which we live is not necessarily found in the subject-object relation, rather, the source of alienation is the fact that humans are, under capitalist relations of production, producing commodities. **And** among those commodities are workers themselves.

> The worker becomes all the poorer the more wealth he produces, the more his production increases in power and size. The worker becomes an ever cheaper commodity the more commodities he creates....Labour produces not only commodities: it produces itself and the worker as commodity--and this in the same general proportion in which it produces commodities.[60]

The specific form objectification takes under capitalism not only involves the separation of the worker from the product of his or her labor, but also the fact that s/he must create his or herself as a **worker** - as a commodity to be sold on the labor market. Thus the laborer and the product of his or her labor come to be treated as the same sorts of **things** - as something produced for the use of another. The result being that workers confront themselves, their own labor and their social relations as alien.

Marx diagnoses the alienation of labor under capitalism along four dimensions as follows:

    1. The worker is alienated from the product of his or her labor. Under capitalism that which the worker produces is not the workers', it is expropriated by the capitalist for exchange and for the capitalist's benefit. Thus the worker confronts the product of labor as something alien.

    2. The worker is alienated from the work process itself. Marx explains:

> But the estrangement is manifested not only in the result but in the **act of production**, within the **producing activity**, itself.... The product is after all but the summary of the activity, of production. If then the product of labour is alienation, production must itself be active alienation, the alienation of activity, the activity of alienation. In the estrangement of the object of labour is merely summarized the estrangement, the alienation, in the activity of labour itself.[61]

How, Marx wonders, would the worker come to be alienated from the product of labor were not the very process of production itself alienated. The worker does not control the process or the means of production. The means, or tools, are owned by the capitalist and the process is imposed by him as well. Thus the worker receives no satisfaction from the labor process under capitalism. This fact is clearly illustrated "in the fact that as soon as no physical or other compulsion exists, labor is shunned like the plague."[62]

3. The worker is alienated from other humans beings, s/he is alienated in her or his social relationships. This is especially true of relationships that directly involve the workplace. The worker must compete in the "free" labor market in order to get a job, compete with other workers in order to win the favor of the bosses, and assist the company in its competition with other companies. As Marx describes it, "within the relationship of estranged labour each man views the other in accordance with the standard and the relationship in which he finds himself as a worker."[63]

4. The worker is alienated from her or his "species being". The German word, "gattungswesen," is used by Feuerbach to identify that which marks humans as a species. In *The Essence of Christianity*, Feuerbach argues that humans are different from other animals in our capacity to think of ourselves as a species having a history and sharing some (unspecified) qualities or concerns. By existing as both an individual and as a group member a human is able to consider "his species,...and not merely his individuality an object of thought."[64] Feuerbach claims that religion (especially Christianity) distracts us from realizing our "species being" because God is naught but an ideal projection of positive human attributes including our hopes for self and species realization. According to religion our salvation will come, if at all, not from ourselves but from God. He believes all this to be unnecessarily mystifying and argues that Christianity could, and should, be transformed into a humanism.[65]

In his analysis of alienated labor Marx takes Feuerbach's account of "species being" as a starting point. Marx agrees that most humans are unaware of the possibility of a species wide conception of history. And, those who are aware are unable to act because of oppressive social conditions.[66] In addition to religion, the primary barriers to awareness and action are ideological, political and economic. Our status as species beings presents the possibility that conscious control of human life, both individual and collective, and free spontaneous activity could be the goal of human life. Capitalism has prevented this from occurring. Marx writes, "[By] degrading spontaneous, free, activity, to a means, estranged labour makes man's species life a means to his physical existence."[67] So, physical existence, which could provide the basis for a free and creative life becomes instead the goal of life.

According to Marx, under capitalism the possibility of we human beings conceiving of ourselves as members of a species with which we might have common concerns is largely blocked.[68] This limits both human capacity for self-realization and the possibilities of revolutionary consciousness.

Workers' alienation under capitalism seems to have two aspects. First, alienation is the suppression, or stunting, of possibilities for human development. Second, the cause of alienation is impersonal and anonymous.

This first general aspect, alienation as suppression is closely tied to Marx's argument that the capitalist organization of labor alienates the worker from species being. As he explains in the *Grundrisse*, labor comes to appear as "mere natural necessity" and not as a function of the individual's own purposes as "self-realization, objectification of the subject, hence real freedom whose action is, precisely labor."[69]

He further explains, in *The German Ideology*, that life is "robbed of real content,"[70] because the capitalist division of labor causes a "one-sided development of one quality at the expense of the rest."[71] Labor comes to be the only quality which is important (because profitable) to develop. For this reason, other aspects of human potential (both individual and collective) are neglected.[72]

More confusing is Marx's claim that alienation which is directed by no subject in particular.[73] What Marx means is i) that the very structure that makes human labor alienating is itself (apparently) beyond human control, and ii) that no single person (or group of people) is responsible for the oppression and alienation. So, not only does labor appear as "mere natural necessity," but so too does the form and cause of oppression. For workers under capitalism,

> the conditions of their life, labour and with it all the conditions of existence in modern society have become something extraneous, something over which they, as separate individuals, have no control, and over which no social organization can give them control.[74]

Among the forms this "alien power" takes are the free labor market, free capitalist competition, the role requirements of the division of labor, and the "illusory community in which individuals have up till now combined" which "always took on an independent existence in relation to them" since it concealed class domination and was thus "for the oppressed class not only a completely illusory community but a new fetter as well."[75]

We are left wondering about the relation between what we might call "objective" and "subjective" alienation. The alienation that Marx describes is supposedly an aspect of every worker's life under capitalism. Under capitalist relations of production, alienation is an objective fact of life. Marx seems to have believed that knowledge of objective alienation could be brought to the attention of consciousness and made subjective. He seems to believe this is possible in spite of his accounts of alienation and fetishism as determining the reach and shape of human consciousness under capitalism. Perhaps he had such hope because the commodification of life was, in the mid-19th century, less far reaching than it is now. This allowed for greater opportunity for lived experience in one part of life to contradict the demands of capitalism. Thus, workers would become aware of their alienation and its structural causes, and then band together in order to overthrow capitalism. Of course, this hasn't happened.[76] A theory of social change which is insufficiently attentive to the possibilities of capitalism to expand to all areas of life, a theory which seems to allow that the subjective conditions for revolution will necessarily follow objective conditions is a theory which seems to warrant the deterministic interpretation held forth by Orthodox Marxism in the 19th and 20th century - the claim that the fall of capitalism is inevitable. Thus we arrive yet again at the "crisis of Marxism."

## Lukacs and Reification

Commodity fetishism is a specific problem of our age.[77]

In *History and Class Consciousness*, Georg Lukacs sets out to answer the problems we've identified as "crisis" of Marxism. Or, more accurately, he sets out to reconstruct a revolutionary Marxism by reviving the Hegelian tradition.[78]

In this attempt he turns to "the question of alienation, which for the first time since Marx is treated as central to the revolutionary critique of capitalism and which has its theoretical and methodological roots in the Hegelian dialectic."[79]

Lukacs was among the first to make use of Marx's early work in informing his understanding of the late "scientific" Marx (i.e.: the Marx of *Capital*). Though he did not have access to *The Economic and Philosophic Manuscripts of 1844*, Lukacs independently arrives at a similar analysis of the alienation of labor. One crucial difference in the accounts is that Lukacs has the benefits of writing "post-*Capital*" and more clearly presents alienation as systemic and structural. By using such early works of Marx as he had access to, Lukacs understands the fetishism of commodities as more than a strictly economic process. Drawing on his reading of Marx's work as an organic whole as well as Weber's analysis of the rationalization of modern society, Hegel's account of the appearance/reality distinction, and Simmel's work on the commodification of culture, Lukacs gives an analysis of how fetishism has extended to the whole of society. This process he calls reification.[80] Reification is an aspect of a form of life unable to understand the material basis of its own institutions and forms of thought.

Max Weber's account of the spread of "rationalization" in the modern world posed an alternative to Marxism that had a marked influence on the work of Lukacs, and later the Frankfurt School. The concept of rationalization appears in many of Weber's writings and refers to a complex set of processes that he finds at work in daily life in modern society. In outline rationalization encompasses: i) the spread of formal rationality, ii) the growing importance of means-ends rationality, and iii) the application of means-ends reasoning to ethical life.[81]

Rationalization takes place along two dimensions. First there was the rationalization of religious thought, what he called the disenchantment of the world. The rationalization of religious thought requires the articulation of a coherent theodicy and a theology capable of explaining every event.[82] As the process continues, religious thought and practice becomes increasingly subject to formal rationality (where the degree of rationality depends upon the degree to which the action is in accord with rationally derivable principles). The rationalization of religion sets the stage for the disenchantment of all aspects of everyday life.[83]

Weber distinguishes formal rationality (which rests upon facts) from substantive rationality (which applies rational calculation to clarify, but not to set or answer, certain goals or questions which involved value judgments). The spread of formal rationality is most clearly exemplified by the extent to which science and scientific principles have come to underlie much of modern life.[84] The process of rationalization had contradictory effects. For one, the rationalization of social life meant that capitalism created the most efficient and productive economic system yet known to humans. Yet, at the same time, the success of this process meant the destruction of the very values in whose name the system was perpetuated; specifically, individual creativity and autonomy. This was accomplished by the spread of formal rationality to areas of social life such as law, the increasing formalization of economic activity, and the rise of modern bureaucracies. As culture became differentiated into different value spheres (art, religion, science, ethics) each sphere progressed according to its own rational principles, but the burden of reconciling the conflicts between value spheres and creating meaning came to rest on each individual. Moreover, as the state and the economy become increasingly subject to formal rationality the possibilities of individuals autonomously creating meaning become stunted.

> This order [the modern economic order] is now bound to the technical and economic conditions of machine production which to-day determine the lives of all the individuals who are born into this mechanism, not only those directly concerned with economic acquisition, with irresistible force.[85]

The rationalization of life in the modern world has created an "iron cage" in which all persons are condemned to live.[86] Attempts to change this situation, especially attempts at socialist revolution, will only further the process of rationalization through the expansion of the bureaucracy.[87]

Lukacs notes that the separation of value spheres identified by Weber appears as the limit of social action under capitalism. In attempts to radically change the system (for Lukacs, class conflict) the boundaries are revealed as historical constructs. In these instances the bourgeoisie react to the declining values and increased barbarism of the age with force. What the bourgeoisie understand as a threatened end to their way of life, the 'best way of life', is abstract human labor power attempting to become concrete through historical action.[88] Although Weber in places recognizes the basis of capitalism in the capitalist organization of labor,[89] in contradistinction to Marx he privileges the notion of formal rationality as the driving force behind rationalization. And, though he lamented the disenchantment of the world, he saw no possibilities of escaping the trajectory laid out by formal reason, no possibility of humans consciously directing history toward their own ends.

Weber's analysis of rationalization as a process whereby economic organization came to shape everyday life was of crucial importance to Lukacs' account of reification.

When Marx wrote his account of the relation between being and consciousness and the role of commodity fetishism under capitalism, his account was limited (mostly) to economic categories, to the world of work. Whereas the account of commodity fetishism was an account of the relations of the work world, Lukacs account of reification is an account of the movement of the commodity form beyond the factory gates and into everyday life (the lifeworld) and in consciousness.

Reification, according to Lukacs, is the process through which human social relations come to appear as relations between things. For example, our society and our history, which are the products of years of activity by millions of humans, appear to be the result of impersonal forces that operate, as do the laws of nature, beyond our control, and finally our understanding. Reification is the application of rationalization to every aspect of life.[90]

One aspect of rationalization is the development of the division of labor and the fragmentation of the production process.[91] These divisions and fragmentations encroach upon the consciousness of the workers who come to understand themselves as "mechanical part[s] incorporated into a mechanical system."[92] Furthermore, the resulting specialization of skills "leads to the destruction of every image of the whole."[93] For this reason, any critique that aims to assist social change must be a total critique and attempt to reimagine a new social whole.

As far as Lukacs is concerned, Marx underestimates the role of subjective conditions in bringing about social change. That is, Marx was not sufficiently aware of the ability of capitalism to control/condition/determine consciousness beyond the factory, nor was he sufficiently aware of the extent to which commodity consciousness could limit the possibilities of revolution. One reason the post-WWI revolutions failed was because the subjective conditions were not right for revolution.

Marx's account of fetishization and the role of ideology as alienated social consciousness explained how and why the social organization of capitalism appears as natural. Lukacs carries this analysis further. Bourgeois consciousness has systematically ignored the distinction between relations of first nature, those relations raised by creative aspects of human need, and second nature, those socially constructed needs that take on a pseudo-objectivity. The confusion works like this. Massive systematic form failures of the present social order appear to consciousness on the same level as natural disasters. To take an example from the culture industry,[94] in the movie *Country* two disasters befall a Midwestern farm family. The first of these is a tornado, the second a bank foreclosure. These two disasters are presented as equal and as natural. Of course, even to consciousness permeated by science-worship as is much of the West, it is easier to conceive of social possibilities where no one will lose their means of subsistence because of a bank foreclosure than to imagine living to see a future where we can control tornadoes. To see a bank foreclosure as natural is to employ reified consciousness.[95]

In the *1844 Manuscripts*, Marx's account of alienation is supposed to be a description of an objective condition of life under capitalist relations of production. Similarly, Lukacs' account of reification is not just an account of subjective experience, rather reification is the reality of life under capitalism. This last phrase, "under capitalism," is important because it reveals that Lukacs conceived of reification as an historically specific reality, one that could, and should, pass away. The failure of bourgeois consciousness to grasp reification as socially and historically specific leads to the antinomies of philosophy.

Reification extends into the theoretical, and supposedly interest free, forms of thought: Philosophy and Science.[96] When Lukacs accords to Philosophy and Science the title "highest forms of thought," he is working within the assumptions of Capitalism. What he will demonstrate is how the socially legitimated intellectual production is reified. In bourgeois science and philosophy, social relations are treated as relations between things. For example, economists talk of "structural unemployment" as an inevitable feature of life. All the time taking little account that the "structurally unemployed" are not just numbers, they are, of course, human beings.

Treating human social relations as relations between things allows the social scientist to formulate laws that govern the movement of 'things' in the system. This means the social sciences should be able to, and often do, accurately predict the actions, motives and movements of human beings. They are successful precisely to the extent that capitalism can succeed in reducing social relations to thing relations. This success of the social sciences, and the appearance of social relations as natural, conceals the fact that if we could see through the appearance, then we could find the possibility of changing the structure of social relations. The objectivity of the social sciences depends upon the stability of the social order in which they exist, the social order that they describe.[97] Failure to realize this, failure to examine the preconceptions of one's own intellectual production is an example of reification at the highest level of thought and culture.

Lukacs considers the philosophy of Kant the highest expression of bourgeois consciousness. Lukacs argues that Kant has done in thought what the bourgeoisie have done in social reality. Kant has sundered reflection on our lives into different spheres (Aesthetic, Religious, Ethical, and Scientific[98]) and privileged the sphere of science. In his *Critique of Pure Reason*, Kant shows the separation of the knowing subject from the object of knowledge, the **ding-an-sich**, the thing-in-itself.

> What our understanding acquires through this concept of a noumenon, is a negative extension that is to say, understanding is not limited through sensibility; on the contrary, it itself limits sensibility by applying the term noumena to things themselves (things not regarded as appearances). But in so doing it at the same time sets limits to itself, recognizing that it cannot know these noumena through any of the categories, and that it must therefore think them only under the title of an unknown something.[99]

The knowing subject, who inhabits the phenomenal world, can never get to the object of knowledge that is in the noumenal world. All that can be known is appearance.

Lukacs, roughly following Marx's analysis of the relation between social being and social consciousness, argues that Kant's epistemology is naught but an expression of the real cleavages in life under capitalism: the cleavages between the bourgeois theorist and labor, the cleavages between human beings,[100] and the cleavages between the laborer and control over the processes of their production. For bourgeois thought, the knowing subject can never reach the object of knowledge because in bourgeois social relations, the bourgeoisie can never reach the object of social production. That is just to say that the bourgeoisie are separated from labor.

For Kant, the antinomies of thought cannot finally be overcome. Against Kant, Hegel argued that the antinomies can be overcome in the final reconciliation of Being with itself. In fact, at times he seems to believe that the end of history is being realized in the specific historical situation in which he lived. As I have discussed earlier in this chapter, much of the subsequent criticism of Hegel accepted his arguments that the antinomies of thought can be overcome through the overcoming of Being's alienation. Where many critics differ with Hegel is on how to understand 'Being'. For Feuerbach (and Heidegger[101]) 'Being' is understood as human being, and human being is conceived of metaphysically, in a manner that leads to the resolution of philosophical antinomies in speculative moral philosophies. Lukacs accepts Marx's arguments that human being is constructed and realized in history. On this account, Being is the history of human practice and only through human practice can the antinomies of thought be dissolved. Through social action we make history "as our history, for their is no other."[102]

If Lukacs is correct, then philosophy, by itself, can never overcome the split between subject and object. Not only Kant, but Fichte, Schiller and Schelling also attempt to overcome the subject/object dualism in the realm of aesthetic reason where practical and intuitive reasoning are joined. Hegel discovers the unfolding of this process in history, but like the theories of his predecessors, Hegel's philosophy "turned back and lost itself in the endless labyrinth of conceptual mythology."[103] These failures are to be expected; since the splits in social reality limit the reach of consciousness, the only way to overcome the "antinomies of bourgeois thought"[104] is to overcome the splits in social life. If philosophy is to assist in this process it must know itself for what it is including its social function. Andrew Feenberg summarizes Lukacs claim: "For Lukacs traditional philosophy is in essence theory of culture that does not know itself as such."[105]

Now Lukacs' critique may not do philosophical justice to Kant's theory. It is however an example of Lukacs' attempts to extend Marx's analysis of bourgeois thought into areas in which it had previously seemed to be ineffective. He is also attempting to show us how to avoid the results of Kant's account, how to avoid conceiving of the subject/object split as inevitable.[106] This is a move both theoretically and politically important for Lukacs to make because,

> classical philosophy finds itself in the historically paradoxical position that it was concerned to find a philosophy that would mean the end of bourgeois society, and to resurrect in thought a humanity destroyed in that society and by it.[107]

According to Lukacs the aim of bourgeois philosophy was to resolve the subject/object split. The only way to do so is for the only potential subject/object to realize itself in history. Since history is the product of human actions, only social action that aims to redirect history toward consciously articulated human goals can hope to realize reason in history. Only historically informed social action can hope to unite the subject and object of history. Lukacs identified the identical subject/object of history as the working class.

As Lukacs argued, the subject/object split is an expression of the splits in social life under capitalism. In order to resolve the theoretical problems, thought alone will not suffice. In order to overcome the theoretical antinomies, the underlying splits in social life must be dissolved. Reified consciousness, which understands the social organization of capitalism as inevitable and conceives of human relationships as relations between things, hides the possibilities of alternative social organization (or, when such alternatives are presented they are framed as 'mere' fantasy). The economic conditions and relations under capitalism demand thought that doesn't make the possibilities of social change conceivable.

The process by which this takes place (the reification of consciousness in everyday life) is not, as it may sound like it is, a conscious conspiracy. The process of reification is part of the structural logic of capitalism. Reification is a process without a subject. No one plans reification, not even the "ruling class" which is itself subject to reified consciousness. One might say the subject is capital itself.

Through the process of reification, capitalism is commodifying the whole of life. Capitalism and the commodity-form and its relations extend far beyond the factory gates. For this reason the practice that resolves the splits in social life must be aimed at the social totality. As capitalism has become a total system and commodified all of life, the critique of capitalism must be not only a critique of the whole, but also a critique that does not itself "freeze once more in a new rigidity and a new immediacy."[108]

Reified consciousness arises from the immediate reality of capitalist society, the omnipresence of the commodity form. To reified consciousness the social relations of capitalism appear as natural. As such, they are but a specific case of a general tendency of theory under capitalism. Reified consciousness treats most general consequences of a historical situation as though they were timeless metaphysical realities. Reified thought "hypothasizes ontologically what is in reality only a dimension of a specific type of [historical/social] practice."[109]

Only by sweeping away the appearance of present social structures as natural can the subjective consciousness necessary to change capitalist social relations arise. So, Lukacs must identify the social location of those able to recognized reified consciousness for what it is. He must identify the cultural location from which the present culture appears not as trans-historical but merely as a historical stage in human history. In order to recognize reified consciousness, the possibility of being not just the object but also the subject of history must exist. In this epistemologically privileged position, "the mysterious impenetrability of the thing-in-itself will be revealed as no more than the illusion of a reified consciousness incapable of recognizing its products."[110] The bourgeoisie and the proletariat experience the immediate reality of capitalism differently. Though both possess reified consciousness, the bourgeoisie feel at home and confirmed by their place in capitalist relations.[111] So, there exists no experiential challenge to their reified belief that this is "the best of all possible worlds."[112] This is in part due to the lack of historical consciousness. To the bourgeoisie, everything about capitalist social relations seems to be understood (or, in principle understandable) except the historical contingency of capitalism itself.[113] All questions can be answered except those about the purpose and origin of the existing social situation. As Fredric Jameson notes, "In this sense, Capitalism is the first thing-in-itself, and the primal contradiction upon which all later, more specialized and abstract dilemmas are founded."[114]

For the proletariat the situation is different. Capitalism, and the universalization of the commodity-form have created an epistemologically privileged position that is occupied by the working class. The economic limits consciousness in that humans can only raise such problems for which it is possible to **imagine** a solution. Under advanced capitalism it is possible to imagine the end of oppressive economic relations. Following Hegel's discussion of Master and Slave, Lukacs argues that this possibility can only be realized by the workers (and those who come to occupy the workers' epistemological position such as certain intellectuals). The immediate reified reality of capitalism is the commodity-form. As worker, the worker knows her or himself as commodity. This is both a theoretical and practical knowledge.

By achieving self-consciousness of her or his status as a commodity, the worker can understand her or himself as the object of capitalism.

Lukacs explains how the realization is possible. As noted above, he argues that no other class can occupy this position. This is because of the nature of productive activity and its organization under capitalism. The product of labor under capitalism appears in the commodity-form. If the worker knows her or himself as commodity, then s/he recognizes her or his position as product of capitalist production. For this reason, the object of production appears not as an impenetrable mystery but as the reality of the workers' social location.

"For the proletariat" writes Lukacs, "however, the 'same' process means **its own emergence as a class.**"[115] The process of reification, the commodification of all aspects of life is the condition for the existence of the proletariat. This process opens up the **possibility** "that workers can become conscious of the social character of labor"[116] thus realizing their position as both the objects of capitalism and the subjects of history.

Lukacs notes, "This enables us to understand why it is only in the proletariat that the process by which a man's achievement is split off from his total personality and becomes a commodity leads to a revolutionary consciousness."[117]

In capitalist relations of production only the proletariat can possibly unite subject and object, although this possibility may be blocked by the difference between "objective" interests in and lived experience of class consciousness. As Lukacs describes the process, freedom and liberation for workers is a determinate negation of the given. Revolutionary social action by the proletariat is not a spontaneous romantic assertion of subjective will, rather it is the realization of potentials that exist, but cannot be actualized within existing society.[118]

Lukacs is arguing that human beings can understand capitalism not as a natural and alienated social formation, but as the material precondition for humans to claim conscious control of our own development.[119] This possibility is limited because fetishized commodity relations have become the basic organizing categories of our experience. As commodity relations extend further into our everyday life (and into our consciousness), our activities (and thoughts) become increasingly oriented toward the reproduction of the system. We are left wondering, if this is the case, then what possibilities for radical social change exist? The gap between potential revolutionary class-consciousness and actual revolution is great.[120]

In the next chapter, I will take up the Frankfurt School's critique of advanced capitalist society. As we shall see, members of the school pick up the Lukacsian model of Marxist cultural critique in their accounts of instrumental reason and technical rationality.

# CHAPTER II

# THE FRANKFURT SCHOOL: THE CRITIQUE OF INSTRUMENTAL RATIONALITY

Science needs those who disobey it.[121]

In the years after Lukacs wrote *History and Class Consciousness* the world saw additional failed revolutions, Marxism used to legitimate the crimes of Stalin, and the rise of Fascism. In this context, the Frankfurt School[122] attempted to continue the project of furthering human liberation through reconstructing Marxism as a 'critical theory' of society with the emphasis on the subjective conditions of revolution.

In the attempt to develop a critical theory, members of the Frankfurt School not only had to address the apparent failings of Marx's theory in history, but also had to articulate a social theory that both contained revolutionary content and took account of the new systems of knowledge that had come to be since Marx's work. What this meant was that they would elaborate a 'critical' Marxism,[123] a version of Marxist theory that was undogmatic and committed more to Marx's project of human liberation than to Marxist orthodoxy as a sacred system of knowledge. In order to accomplish this they supplemented their Marxist perspective with the findings of other viewpoints and enriched it by approaching social theory from an interdisciplinary perspective. Thus, we find critical theory drawing upon anthropology, sociology and psychology, Marxist intellectual and political traditions, as well as the work of Freud and Weber.

## Horkheimer and Adorno: The Critique Of Instrumental Reason

Man imagines himself free from fear when there is no longer anything unknown. . . . Enlightenment is mythic fear turned rational.[124]

The Frankfurt School program in the 1930s was to develop a concept of reason as a critical tool that could be used to critique existing society and the instrumental reason that justified it. As explained by Horkheimer, philosophy was to be set free from its existing forms as either "Idealism" or "Naturalism"[125] in order that its critical potential be realized. Philosophy thus realized as a critical theory could then be employed to locate the contradictions in society and addressed to potential revolutionary subjects as an articulation of their lived experience.

The method of critical theory was to be one of immanent critique. Employed in critique, the method identifies the self-proclaimed ideals of a theory (or society) and contrasts them with the actually existing conditions. This is an attempt to realize Hegel's theory of history in conscious practice. In the first step of constructing a critical philosophy, "philosophy confronts the existent, in its historical context, with the claim of its conceptual principles, in order to criticize the relation between the two and thus transcend them."[126]

Following this same model, articulating the ideals of a situation and confronting them with the existing reality, critical theory can construct a critique of capitalist society. The bourgeois revolutions were fought in the name of certain ideals (liberty, equality, justice) that have not been realized in social reality. Reason, broadly considered, demands that a society embody the ideals it speaks, and when it doesn't, a gap is opened. Those who fall into this gap, that is, those whose lived experience is not one of freedom and equality are, following Lukacs, the potential revolutionary subjects. By addressing the theory to them, they are given a tool to aid their struggle for a rational society, a society that lives up to its own ideals.[127]

When Horkheimer and Adorno turn their attention to a critique of instrumental reason,[128] the goal is to overcome the subjective constraints on creating just such a rational society. The theory will ultimately be judged as to its success in enlightening members of its audience as to the reality of their situation and their role in transforming the situation.[129]

By the late 1940s, Horkheimer and Adorno became increasingly pessimistic about the possibilities for a class-based revolution and looked increasingly to a critique of philosophy and culture for locating possibilities of human liberation.

In light of the pessimism found in their later work, as well as the apparent lack of concern with revolutionary action, it is helpful to turn to early essays by Horkheimer and Adorno in order to uncover explicit ties to the Western Marxist tradition, including the belief that, at some level, economic crisis is a necessary though not sufficient condition for the overthrow of capitalism.

In "Traditional and Critical Theory", Horkheimer writes:

> Because of its situation in modern society the proletariat experiences the connection between work which puts ever more powerful instruments into men's hands in their struggle with nature, and the continuous renewal of an outmoded social organization.... Production is not geared to the life of the whole community while heeding also the claims of individuals; it is geared to the power-packed claims of individuals while being concerned hardly at all with the life of the community.[130]

It is only by challenging and abolishing capitalist relations of production that human liberation might be achieved. And, following Lukacs, Horkheimer identifies the proletariat as the class whose experiences make it possible to grasp the nature of the present society. Progress in the forces of production has created objective possibilities for human liberation. These possibilities have not yet been realized. He continues:

> But it must be added that even the situation of the proletariat is, in this society, no guarantee of correct knowledge. The proletariat may indeed have experience of meaninglessness in the form of continuing and increasing wretchedness and injustice in its own life.[131]

In this passage Horkheimer acknowledges the role of consciousness in radical social change, as well as the necessity of the correct economic conditions. Drawing on Lukacs' account of reification, he argues that even the proletariat, the social class within capitalism capable of realizing its position **and** the identity of its interests with those of society as a whole, will "fall into slavish dependence on the status quo."[132]

It is against this background, and the advent and rise to power of fascism in Europe, that Horkheimer and Adorno undertake their analysis and critique of the nature and role of reason in the history of the West. Their goal is to provide an analysis, at the level of consciousness and theory, of the conditions that exist and function to limit the progress of human liberation.

Neither Adorno nor Horkheimer has much faith that the meaning of history, understood in Hegelian terms, can be realized. Adorno explains: "After the catastrophes that have happened, and in view of the catastrophes to come, it would be cynical to say that a plan for a better world is manifested in history and unites it."[133]

Horkheimer and Adorno do not believe the suffering of past generations can be redeemed by any future totalization, by any future identity of subject and object. In this, they are breaking with the utopian hopes that can be traced through the work of Hegel, Marx and Lukacs.[134]

When Horkheimer and Adorno look about, they cannot identify any potential revolutionary subject-object of history. Further, they find attempts at subject-object identity, attempts to build new social totalities as tending toward authoritarianism. In attempts to conceptualize the whole, to "think the totality,"[135] they find attempts to dissolve all differences, freeze the object of history, and ignore its particularities and history. Such attempts are attempts to destroy otherness and thereby destroy fear. The desire to control the world and fear of chaos underlies all philosophical systems in so far as they lay claim to absolute knowledge of the world.

> This fear shaped the beginnings of a mode of conduct constitutive for bourgeois existence as a whole: of the neutralization, by confirming the existent order, of every emancipatory step. In the shadow of its own incomplete emancipation the bourgeois consciousness must fear to be annulled by a more advanced consciousness; not being the whole freedom, it senses it can only produce a caricature of freedom--hence its theoretical expansion of its autonomy into a system similar to its own coercive mechanisms.[136]

In tearing down the old world order, the bourgeois revolutions presented the possibility of a world without order, of chaos. In the process of imposing order in this world, bourgeois consciousness in practice was unable to realize the full liberation in the name of which the revolutions were carried out. Adorno, following Marx, believes this failure is due primarily to the organization of production and thus the entirety of life in bourgeois society. That is, the reason the bourgeois revolutions could not realize their self-proclaimed ideals is because they were also revolutions in the name of capital.[137] So, in order to achieve an ordered world and in order to ameliorate its fear of being replaced by consciousness that might be capable of, in practice, achieving a greater degree of human freedom, bourgeois consciousness engages in the construction of great systems that claim to represent the totality. Such systems present themselves as orderly pictures of the whole of reality and as such tolerate nothing outside of themselves.[138]

Constructing this sort of totalizing system, Horkheimer and Adorno argue, has been the Western intellectual project. And though usually identified with the Enlightenment, Adorno and Horkheimer trace the roots of this project as far back as Odysseus.[139]

In *Dialectic of Enlightenment* they argue that the desire for a total system, for an identity of subject and object is motivated by fear of chaos (and fear of 'the other') in a non-totalizable world and fear of impotence to act in the world. Attempts to bring subject and object together attempt to assuage these fears by subsuming the object in the subject.

In advanced (state) capitalism the powers that be distrust critical questioning and dissent. In response they (the state, the corporation) take recourse to terror (union busting, beating suspects) and coercion (IMF) to enforce the program of 'progress' legitimated by a blind faith in historical progress. Through this process, our lives become dissolved in administration. We become machines of repetitive production (work) and repetitive mass consumption (leisure). Advanced capitalism is a global phenomenon that received a clear articulation in the Enlightenment divisions of subject and object (Descartes), and spirit and matter (Newton).

In traditional conceptions of the movement of the dialectic, in history or in thought, each moment in the dialectic can overcome all oppositions as it progresses to the next moment and a new synthesis. This is the standard interpretation of the dialectic found in Hegel, Marx and Lukacs, the dialectic progresses by transcending present moments to new totalizing syntheses that retain the truth of the earlier moments.

Adorno and Horkheimer argue that while subject and object do constitute each other, they cannot be reduced to any identity. To identify one with the other is to produce, in thought, a false identity. The tendency in social organization toward total organization and reduction of all humans to equivalents is a practical counterpart to thinking a false identity, it is, as we shall see, the outcome of valorizing instrumental reason. These totalizing systems (such a corporate and governmental bureaucracies) produce within themselves what bourgeois society has not produced within social life: stability, and the ability to consciously and rationally direct our lives. Of course, this rationality is in some ways only apparent -- it doesn't extend beyond these systems, hence the critique of instrumental reason.[140]

The effort to conceptualize the whole tolerates nothing outside itself. But, such systems inevitably enter into conflict with the objectivity they claim to grasp. Horkheimer and Adorno argue that history defies systems and the qualitatively differentiated particulars will reassert themselves to contradict the system.[141] What this means is that in so far as theory claims to present the correct or 'true' description of the world, and in so far as theory presents an ordered and total picture, and if the world is not orderly, then the disorder of the world will conflict with the theory. This will occur by the resistance of particulars (events, processes, lives) that resist the reified description imposed by theory. The particular can be salvaged, argue Horkheimer and Adorno, through remembrance.[142] Through remembrance the particular can be salvaged and the hold of total systematic rationality can be broken and a space for freedom and creativity can open.

Identity thinking obscures the possibility of freedom by reducing qualitatively differentiated particulars to equivalents by subsuming all in the totality. Efforts at subject-object identity are examples of bourgeois economism, i.e.: examples of reified thought. Adorno and Horkheimer hold that such thinking cannot penetrate the reified world of appearances to grasp the non-identity of the underlying reality. So, any critical theory which aims at subject-object identity will fail to recognize the diversity of life-forms which it aims to assist in liberation. Actions undertaken in the name of such theory may be organized in such a way as to destroy within the movement the very freedom and diversity at which they aim.

Attempts at subject-object identity work to fulfill the desire for stability and thereby serve a legitimation function for the authoritarian state.[143] As the shape of capitalism has changed, become increasingly interlocked and multinational, the particular has increasingly been under assault. The goal and function of multinational capital and international marketing (the universalization of exchange) is to create a single world market (IMF, NAFTA, EU, GATT, and so on). Though the appearance is one of growing market differentiation, the effect is to reduce the cultural and historical specificity of different situations to a single dimension that can be grasped by technical rationality, what Horkheimer and Adorno call "Instrumental Reason."

> The exchange principle, the reduction of human labour to its abstract universal concept of average labour-time, is fundamentally related to the principle of identification. Identification has its social model in exchange and exchange would be nothing without it.[144]

In such a situation identity thinking is counterrevolutionary as its primary function is not to challenge but to justify the trajectory which capitalism is taking.

In general outline, this is the argument advanced by Adorno and Horkheimer. They focus particular attention on a critique of instrumental reason.

*Dialectic of Enlightenment* is one of the central texts in understanding the Frankfurt school. In this work Adorno and Horkheimer lay out their account of the rise of instrumental reason and the dialectic between the Enlightenment and enlightenment. They explain the dialectic of Enlightenment reason:

> As the transcendental supraindividual self, reason comprises the idea of a free, human social life in which men organize themselves as the universal subject and overcome the conflict between pure and empirical reason in the conscious solidarity of the whole. This represents the idea of true universality: utopia. At the same time, however, reason constitutes the court of judgment of calculation, which adjusts the world for the ends of self-preservation and recognizes no function other than the preparation of the object from mere sensory material in order to make it the material of subjugation.[145]

The Enlightenment's conception of reason reveals these contradictory moments: First, reason is universal and demands autonomy and liberation. Yet, at the same time, reason is interested in the rationalization of social structures and domination of nature.

The structure of enlightenment also reveals contradictions. On the one hand it is liberating reason, freeing humans from domination and oppression. On the other, enlightened thought tends to aspire to totality, to absolute status whereby it becomes a new force of oppression. As they write, "myth is already enlightenment, and enlightenment reverts to myth."[146]

With the expansion of capitalism and bureaucracies, both public and private, reason becomes unable to engage in critical thinking about society; "objectified thinking cannot even raise the problem."[147] The very nature of Enlightenment thought in action requires this limitation on the reach of reason.

Horkheimer and Adorno argue that in modern industrial society instrumental reason comes to play the role of Reason itself. That is, reasoning where i) the means are subordinated to the ends, ii) the ends themselves come to be outside the conversation, or iii) perpetuating the means becomes the end, comes to dominate. In such a situation all we can discuss is method.

> Bourgeois society is ruled by equivalence. It makes the dissimilar comparable by reducing it to abstract quantities. To the Enlightenment, that which does not reduce to numbers, and ultimately to the one, becomes illusion; modern positivism writes it off as literature. Unity is the slogan from Parminides to Russell. The destruction of gods and qualities alike is insisted upon.[148]

While it is the nature of instrumental reason to attempt to comprehend everything in mathematical terms, and to reject that which it cannot, it would be a mistake to believe, as some commentators have,[149] that this is the characteristic of instrumental reason which Horkheimer and Adorno believe necessarily leads to domination. As they explain: "Its untruth does not consist in what its romantic enemies have always reproached it for: analytical method, return to elements, dissolution through reflective thought; but instead in the fact that for enlightenment the process is always decided from the start."[150]

So, what appears as a new fear, a fear of all that cannot be quantified, calculated or manipulated under some mathematical model, is an old fear in a new guise. Instrumental reason functions to contain the fear of the unknown by having predetermined ends. The means to these ends can be objectively and rationally justified by appeal to the methods of instrumental reason. As noted above, any thought that cannot be explicated in these terms is considered irrational and therefore suspect. Thus, the possibilities of critical thought are ruled out from the start. This is true, although in different ways, of both private capitalism and state capitalism.[151]

According to Horkheimer and Adorno, capitalism in all of its guises moves aside older aristocratic cultural forms and ways of thinking. One cannot analyze and hope to understand fascism without also discussing its relations to the logic of capitalism as state capitalism. Both private and state capitalism lead to the manipulation of culture and the narrowing of critical reasoning. Although in importantly different ways, this was true, they argue, in both Western democracies and in the failed attempts at totalitarian states in Germany, Italy, Spain and the USSR.[152] Through this critique of how Enlightenment thought which aimed at human liberation comes to function as a new force for domination, Horkheimer and Adorno offer the provocative argument that Western reason itself is also a force of domination and destruction. Such reason attempts to destroy the specificity of individuals and to destroy the otherness of the other.

In an era when instrumental considerations dominate, "[t]he conception of unfettered activity, of uninterrupted procreation, of chubby insatiability, of freedom as frantic bustle, feeds on the bourgeois concept of nature that has always served solely to proclaim social violence as unchangeable, as a piece of healthy eternity."[153] In this passage, Adorno is recounting, and lamenting, the manner in which Enlightenment ideal of freedom has come to mean activity that perpetuates existing conditions under the guise of 'progress' and 'human nature'. One of the aspects of modern society that enables this perverse conception of freedom is mass culture.[154]

In *Dialectic of Enlightenment*, Horkheimer and Adorno offer a critique of 'the culture industry' as the means of popular mass deception. In response to the changing form of popular culture in the early and mid-twentieth century, they offer a through and total critique of popular culture that presents members of the working class as naive victims of capitalist manipulation. Because of their account of mass culture as effectively engineering the commodification of non-work time[155], and because of their general pessimism about the possibility of radical change in late capitalist culture, Horkheimer and Adorno are often charged with a form of cultural elitism and being "hostile to human beings as they are."[156] Adorno explains, quoting Horkheimer:

> We criticize mass culture not because it gives men too much or makes their life too secure - that we leave to Lutheran theology - but rather because it contributes to a condition in which men get too little and what they get is bad, a condition in which whole strata inside and out live in frightful poverty, in which men come to terms with injustice, in which the world is kept in a condition where one must expect on the one hand giant catastrophes and on the other clever elites conspiring to bring about a dubious peace.[157]

Horkheimer and Adorno critique mass culture for the same reasons which they critique any other aspect of late capitalist culture. Accepting the way things are blocks the possibility of considering alternatives. The argument is similar to that offered by Horkheimer in "Traditional and Critical Theory," accepting existing cultural forms without critical reflection is to be complicit with existing culture and to assist its continued existence.[158]

The charges of elitism are also directed at the style of their work, especially that of Adorno.[159] And, it is true that reading Adorno's work is no simple task. Herbert Marcuse defended his friend:

> His language is excessive because of the fear of succumbing to reification, . . . the fear of being too easily understood and becoming familiar and therefore misunderstood. I must admit that Adorno's sentences have often enraged me, . . . but I think that is what they're supposed to do. And I don't think I need be ashamed of it.[160]

The very style in which Adorno wrote was an attempt to avoid an uncritical reading. It is not possible to read Adorno and understand him without engaging in a length interaction with the text and a period of self-reflection.[161] The complexities and contradictions of modern life which concerned Adorno often could not be explained simply, and when they could a simple explanation might lead one to believe that s/he completely understood the problem. But, this sort of reduction of the complexities of life is precisely one of the characteristics of instrumental rationality which Adorno contested in everything he wrote, in part because simple reductive descriptions and explanations allow one to gloss over the underlying contradictions.

Adorno is attempting, best as he can given the circumstances, to construct a counter-hegemonic discourse while separated from active political movements. Perhaps it is for this reason that Adorno tends to ignore existing working class resistance and downplays the very real gains won by many people in their struggle with the ruling class. Nancy

Fraser's attempts to outline a socialist-feminism suggest that mechanisms exist for concretely realizing the necessarily complex discourse needed to both i) give a 'thick' description of our present situation, and ii) articulate positive alternatives. That is, she urges us to realize in our political culture that which Adorno realizes in his philosophical discourse.[162]

All of this suggests, correctly I think, that throughout their work, Horkheimer and Adorno contest the notion of freedom as choice between brands of toothpaste, and the notion of reason as determining how best to prosecute a war or raise profits. They never give up the hope (especially Adorno), no matter how obscure it seems in their work, that the future can be different and more free than the present. In other words, Horkheimer and Adorno wish to "save the Enlightenment from itself and preserve its goal of human liberation."[163]

## The Positivist Dispute: The Critique Of Instrumental Reason in Practice

Progress is leaving itself behind.[164]

In order to understand what it would mean to "save the Enlightenment from itself" we need to acknowledge that Horkheimer and Adorno's discussion of instrumental reason is not completely critical. The use of instrumental reason initially had the effect of liberating humans from dogma and illusion.[165] Furthermore, during the Enlightenment there was a certain moral motivation underlying the use of instrumental reason to critique existing social and intellectual edifices.[166] The point of the critique was to allow human beings to escape the domination of nature and to overcome the necessity of labor.[167] And, we should recall that the successes of the physical and natural sciences in the 18th and 19th centuries seemed to justify optimism that their procedures might be applied in the human sciences. However, Horkheimer and Adorno argue that in the 20th century as the triumph of the Enlightenment has become near total, the use of instrumental reason has come to block the possibility of a critical theory of society which might further the cause of human liberation. This is what they mean when they write:

> If it [Enlightenment thought triumphant] willingly emerges from its critical element to become a mere means at the disposal of the existing order, then despite itself it tends to convert the positive it elected to defend into something negative and destructive.[168]

They locate this trend in what they call "positivism." Positivism, as they understand it, is a stance of skeptical empiricism that holds that fact and value are distinct, sensory experience is of discreet particulars, and that sense experience is the ultimate source of knowledge. Since fact and value are completely distinct, this knowledge will be objective and systematic. Horkheimer and Adorno note that from this follows "the impossibility of deriving from reason any fundamental argument against murder."[169]

Horkheimer and Adorno argue that this conception is highly problematic in general. What has taken place is a confusion of knowledge of facts with knowledge of reality. This confusion betrays a forgetting, a forgetting of the Enlightenment's own history, specifically Kant's demonstration that the world "is partially the result of the workings of our understanding."[170] What they are arguing is that experience of the given is mediated by consciousness. But, as Horkheimer explains:

> Even this view is too narrow. In order to place man's present consciousness of facts in their right context, it is not sufficient to trace the abstract principle of the ego in its historical interconnections. The opposition of the ego and the world, in its definite form, belongs to a transitory historical epoch.... The facts of science and science itself are but segments of the life process of society, and in order to understand the significance of facts or of science generally one must possess the key to the historical situation, the right social theory.[171]

Drawing on Hegel's insight that the content of consciousness is determined by the historical situation, together with the understanding of experience as mediated by consciousness; Horkheimer and Adorno argue that the process of knowing cannot be separated from its historical conditions. "Things" come to us embedded in relations and can only be understood in that context.[172] We should note that part of that context is the situation of the 'knower', that is, our situation that too will be historically variable. This is what Horkheimer meant when he claimed that to understand the world we must understand ourselves.

If all this is correct, then theorists cannot remain detached and objective because they too are embedded in historically constructed

social relations. This means that claims to 'objectivity' or to a viewpoint outside the matter under investigation are mistaken. The claims of modern science to objectivity are illusory.[173]
Under the influence of positivism, consciousness comes to objectify the social as well as the natural world. This means that the entire world is conceived as a world of objects subject to manipulation and a human being is considered to be "an isolated object, a set of physical events like any other."[174]

Society appears to positivist consciousness reified as second nature: the norms, customs, regularities and laws of society are considered as natural. When understood as being natural, social facts and historical laws are considered immutable and beyond our control. Such thinking forgets that history, though subject to 'laws', is made by human beings and its laws are the product of a particular historical situation.[175]

These 'laws', which appear to govern social reality, are not illusory. Horkheimer and Adorno explain that in a world governed by exchange relations and characterized by capitalist relations of production the whole of life becomes commodified.

> The economic apparatus, even before total planning, equips commodities with the values which decide human behavior. Since with the end of free exchange, commodities lost all their economic qualities except for fetishism, the latter has extended its arthritic influence over all aspects of social life.[176]

In order to survive in this world, individuals must be as commodities. As such, individuals and their relations appear to be describable by laws. So, theory that describes this world and its 'laws' is correct. But, such theory does not engage critically with its object, instead positivist theory duplicates the reified thinking of the social order studied. And, the fact that the theory correctly predicts social events should not "delude the theoretician that he has penetrated society."[177] Rather, such theory has confused social and natural processes, and has a confused understanding of nature that is often predictable only in so far as we can control it. Some of the results of positivist thinking are a fetishization of the status quo, a loss of the particular, and a closing off of consideration of alternative social arrangements. If what exists is as it is because it is the product of inexorable historical forces, then what purpose is served by thinking of alternatives?

Marcuse also takes up the critique of positivism. And, like Horkheimer and Adorno, he wishes to preserve a space for alternatives, for the imaginary to play a role in critical social theory. His clearest discussion of positivism is found in *Reason and Revolution*. In positivist social theory, specifically that of Auguste Comte, human beings and human social organization are treated as value neutral objects about which scientific investigation will yield facts. Any other considerations are digressions into 'transcendental illusions.' Consequently,

> [t]he new sociology is to tie itself to the facts of the existing social order and, though it will not reject the need for correction and improvement, it will exclude any move to overthrow or negate that order. As a result, the conceptual interest of positive sociology is to be apologetic and justificatory.[178]

The function of positive sociology is to study the existing society on the grounds and in the terms set by the society itself. Such a social theory might recognize the need for reform, but even the nature of reform will be dictated by the "machinery of the established order."[179]

One of the uses of this 'new sociology' is to remove many issues from the realm of social struggle and submit them to analysis by experts whose methodology is determined by the desire to perpetuate existing structures and whose consciousness is limited to consideration of the existent.

We should note that positivism claims to be a theory which is value free appealing only to 'the facts'. But, in claiming that the imaginary can serve no legitimate role in social criticism, positivism claims that what is, is what ought to be. This smuggled in value claim is one which positivism cannot justify.[180]

According to Marcuse, what positivist social theory has forgotten is the above-mentioned character of history as made by human beings. Since societies are in history and depend upon the everyday life and consciousness of human beings for their reproduction, the possibility exists that humans might decide to seize control of history and remake social relations. As we shall see Marcuse attempts to retain this positive, utopian moment in the Marxist dialectic.[181]

## Marcuse: The Critique of Science and the Search for Revolutionary Subjects

Free election of masters does not abolish the masters or the slaves. Free choice among a wide variety of goods and services does not signify freedom if these goods and services sustain controls over a life of toil and fear--that is, if they sustain alienation. And the spontaneous reproduction of superimposed needs by the individual does not establish autonomy; it only testifies to the efficacy of the controls.[182]

Herbert Marcuse's work on the role of technical rationality in creating 'one dimensional society', was not only an important conduit of radical thought to many in the 'New Left' in the 1960s, his work was also an important and original attempt to reformulate Marxism in what he called advanced industrial society.[183] In order to understand his analysis in *One Dimensional Man*, it is helpful to examine his early writings on the role of science and technology.

As Marcuse notes, from the Enlightenment thought of the 16th and 17th centuries comes the notion that the individual is rational, creative and capable of independent thinking and autonomous action. In order that such an individual be fulfilled, be able to realize her/his potential, certain economic and social conditions had to be met. According to bourgeois thought, these conditions include free and open competition in the market, and liberalism in political organization. But, over time the relations within capitalist production begin to reveal economic individualism as a facade of capitalism. The production of commodities, including workers, undermines the economic and cultural basis that creates the possibility of autonomous individuals by increasingly demanding submission to technical rationality. Capitalism is not economic democracy. As critical reason becomes more and more attenuated, the possibility of articulating alternatives to the present state of affairs drops away, or at least appears as irrational (thus to articulate such alternatives is possible, **but** to do so is to be engaged in the production of naught but fantasy which can, of course, never be realized).[184] This was Marcuse's analysis of modern industrial society that he characterized as 'one-dimensional'.

As Marcuse explains it, the process works like this: Industry becomes organized so that individual achievement is measured in terms of production. And, reminiscent of Marx on the alienation of labor, Marcuse notes that individual performance comes to be judged by standards external to both the individual and the production process.[185]

The growth of forces of production, along the lines dictated by instrumental reason, what Marcuse calls technical rationality, come to create "a set of truth values which hold good for the functioning of the apparatus--and for that alone."[186]

In such a situation, if a worker desires to maintain her or his own life, then s/he must act rationally. But, what counts as rational is define, by the apparatus as whatever will perpetuate presently existing conditions. In this manner do means of control become internalized and appear to the individual as the dictates of reason itself. And, thus does critical thinking become increasingly difficult.[187]

Like Lukacs, Horkheimer and Adorno, Marcuse argues that Marx's writings provide an account of consciousness and ideology that is inadequate to understanding the efficacy of capitalism in thwarting crisis by integrating the needs and interests of the working class into those of capital. This is in large part because Marx focused his work on production[188] and because he lived before the advent of the 'consciousness industry'.[189]

In *One Dimensional Man*, Marcuse sets out "An attempt to recapture the critical intent of these categories [class, private, individual]."[190] As such,

> *One Dimensional Man* will vacillate throughout between two contradictory hypotheses: (1) that advanced industrial society is capable of containing qualitative change for the foreseeable future; (2) that forces and tendencies exist which may break this containment and explode the society.[191]

There are passages throughout Marcuse's writings that indicate he shared the pessimism of Horkheimer and Adorno and saw the first hypothesis as correct.[192] Yet, he never abandons the hope that conditions might be otherwise, that the second tendency might become dominant.[193] If that is to be the case, then new human beings must be created, humans whose desires and needs have not been shaped and directed by interests other than their own, beings with some autonomy with regards to evaluating and choosing their desires. Marcuse argues that the role of philosophy is to assist this change:

> The philosophical construction of reason is replace by the creation of a rational society. The philosophical ideals of a better world and of true Being are incorporated into the practical aim of struggling mankind, where they take on a human form.[194]

Marcuse realized that since the historical situation has changed since Marx and Lukacs wrote (and even since *Dialectic of Enlightenment*) he would have to provide a new analysis of the forces which make up advanced capitalist society. He argues, "that this society is irrational as a whole. Its productivity is destructive of the free development of human needs and faculties."[195]

Advanced capitalism rests upon a development of productive forces the like of which has not been seen heretofore. The explosion of productive forces is the result of developments in science and technology and depends upon an increasing concentration of capital. This process is furthered by the transfer of ownership of the means of production from individual capitalists to corporate capital that actually allows more concentration while appearing to avoid the evils of the "robber baron" capitalists.[196] In this way the 'subject' of capitalism becomes harder to identify. These changes demand increasing automation and productivity[197] and more scientific management that leads to larger private bureaucracies.[198]

As we might expect, central to Marcuse's analysis/critique of advanced capitalist society is the notion that the commodity form has come to be far more pervasive than Marx ever envisaged. Drawing largely on Marx's *Economic and Philosophic Manuscripts of 1844* and Lukac's *History and Class Consciousness*, Marcuse argues that the commodity form, along with the rise in consumerism, has a stabilizing effect upon the capitalist mode of production by, in effect, creating new types of individuals.

> The people recognize themselves in their commodities; they find their soul in their automobile, hi-fi set, split-level home, kitchen equipment. The very mechanism which ties the individual to his society has changed, and social control is anchored in the new needs it has produced.[199]

What is 'new' about these individuals (us) is the new needs and values produced by 'one-dimensional society.' These needs are those that the society is already prepared to satisfy and function to integrate the individual into the society. Thus, they serve to contain the possibility of radical social change.

The new needs constructed in late capitalism, what Marcuse will call 'false needs' are produced not just by the obvious sources, advertising and the culture industry, but also by the very organization of the forces of production. In a passage which draws on Adorno's critique of instrumental reason Marcuse explains,

> [I]n a specific sense advanced industrial society is **more** ideological than its predecessor, inasmuch as today the ideology is in the process of production itself. In a provocative form, this proposition reveals the political aspects of the prevailing technological rationality. The productive apparatus and the goods and services which it produces "sell" or impose the social system as a whole. The means of mass transportation and communication, the commodities of lodging, food, and clothing, the irresistible output of the entertainment and information industry carry with them prescribed attitudes and habits, certain intellectual and emotional reactions which bind the consumers more or less pleasantly to the producers and, through the latter, to the whole. The products indoctrinate and manipulate; they promote a false consciousness which is immune against its falsehood. And as these beneficial products become available to more individuals in more social classes, the indoctrination they carry ceases to be publicity; it becomes a way of life. It is a good way of life-- much better than before--and as a good way of life, it militates against qualitative change. Thus emerges a pattern of **one-dimensional thought** and **behavior** in which ideas, aspirations, and objectives that, by their content, transcend the established universe of discourse and action are either repelled or reduced to terms of this universe.[200]

Marcuse argues that beyond biological needs, all human needs are constructed in historical situations and conditioned by existing social structures.[201] Nonetheless, he distinguishes between 'true' and 'false' needs. True needs are those that are essential for human survival the satisfaction of which is a precondition for the satisfaction of all other needs.

> "False" [needs] are those which are superimposed upon the individual by particular social interests in his repression: the needs which perpetuate toil, aggressiveness, misery, and injustice.... Such needs have a societal content and function which are determined by external powers over which the individual has no control.[202]

"False" needs are false not because they do not originate in part of some essential human nature, but because their origin and function is in the repression of an individual's free and conscious creation of a life. False needs hold out the promise that their gratification will lead to happiness, an interesting lifestyle, "successful" relations with one's choice of sex partners, youthfulness, and individuality. The path to realizing these is usually through the purchase of a particular commodity.[203] As Doug Kellner has written: "[If a] commodity fails to offer the satisfactions promised and is not beneficial, life enhancing and useful, but is, on the contrary, poorly constructed, over-priced or not really useful, then a perceived need for it can be said to be a 'false need'."[204]

According to Marcuse even a way of life becomes a thing, a commodity to be purchased and which may be acquired and discarded at will--that is, if one but has sufficient financial resources. Attempts to satisfy these needs bind the individual to the existing social order, and cannot, ultimately be fulfilled. The culture makes 'false promises'.[205]

Images of people individually fulfilling these desires flood the market. Groups, or individuals as members of a group are not shown fulfilling collective desires. Nor are they shown fulfilling individual (or collective) desires collectively, which may be the only way to satisfy these desires. The separateness of desire satisfaction presented by capitalism serves to reinforce the competition necessary even to hope to obtain some of the products or lifestyles.

By contrast, satisfaction of true needs can allow for "the optimal development of the individual."[206] For an individual, the question of whether a need is true or false can only be answered by the individual, but s/he must be an autonomous individual not constrained by the false needs whose purpose is to further a repressive social system. This leaves Marcuse with a question:

> How can the people who have been the object of effective and productive domination by themselves create the conditions of freedom? The more rational, productive, technical, and total the regressive administration of society becomes, the more unimaginable the means and ways by which the administered individuals might break their servitude and seize their own liberation.[207]

At this point Marcuse, like Horkheimer and Adorno, seems caught in a pessimism about the possibilities of change. Modern technological society has created such abundance that the proletariat has been completely integrated into "a monolithic social order of oppression and conformity."[208] Furthermore, as suggested by the headnote to this section, the masses now freely elect their (our?) masters. The technological and economic capacity for freedom, or at least more freedom, exist in the "first world", so "false needs" are very important to maintaining social order and control.

Missing from this account of modern life is any account of resistance. Stanley Aronowitz is critical of Marcuse for ignoring working class resistance to the one-dimensional society. Aronowitz emphasizes the resistance present in everyday life, in the structure of our relationships with other people. According to Aronowitz, the reification of aspects of working class life will meet with resistance. This resistance might not be immediately politically effective against oppressive structures, but the very fact of resistance means that the possibility of revolution is not completely extinguished in advanced capitalism.[209]

Marcuse does acknowledge the continued possibility of challenges to, and crises of, the social system. Of all the first generation Critical Theorists, only Marcuse maintained an intransigently revolutionary politics and a connection to existing political movements.[210]

One part of Marcuse's analysis is found in *Counterrevolution and Revolt*. In this text he argues that not only does consumer society produce needs, but it produces surplus needs just as it produces surplus value or surplus inventory of consumer items. As noted above, the character of some of these needs may be such that they cannot be satisfied by individualized consumption. Desire is restless, and the manner in which capitalism produces needs that cannot be satisfied only deepens and encourages this restlessness. Furthermore, part of the marketing of products in advanced capitalism is through constructions of happiness and the good life. Yet, during eras of economic downturn, the consumer society may not be able to satisfy these needs. And, at all times the society will fail to satisfy some of these desires for some people. In fact, if Marcuse is correct, capitalism needs some unsatisfied desires -- they provide impetus to produce and consume. At the same time, unsatisfied desires can be sources for individual dis-ease and social unrest. In this way, the very process necessary for the continuation of the system will pose a threat to the system.[211] Not exactly the sort of class-based analysis that Aronowitz offered, but Marcuse does demonstrate an understanding of the continuing role of the economy in shaping the terrain for struggle.[212]

After, and in part in response to, the revolts of the 1960s, Marcuse offers an account of the social locations of potential revolutionary agents. In *One Dimensional Man*, he argues that:

## The Frankfurt School: The Critique of Instrumental Rationality

> The struggle for the solution has outgrown the traditional forms. . . . However, underneath the conservative popular base is the substratum of outcasts and outsiders, the exploited and persecuted of other races and other colors, the unemployed and the unemployable.... [T]heir opposition is revolutionary even if their consciousness is not.[213]

Here Marcuse is arguing that the traditional form of struggle valorized by many Marxists, the revolution of the industrial working class, is an unlikely occurrence. In large part because the working class in advanced capitalism has been well integrated into the system and often members of the working class understand maintaining the status quo as being in their interest. Marcuse locates resistance at the 'margins' of society.[214]

According to Marx, revolutionary consciousness was determined by material conditions. For Marcuse, revolutionary consciousness requires education[215] and total refusal of the values of the system. We cannot know, beforehand, who will play the role of revolutionary agents. This is one reason for the importance of education -- all must be prepared to play a role in social transformation. This includes developing critical and autonomous reasoning skills. In *An Essay on Liberation* Marcuse writes:

> The search for specific historical agents of revolutionary change in the advanced capitalist countries is indeed meaningless. Revolutionary forces emerge in the process of change itself; the translation of the potential to the actual is the work of political practice.[216]

All critical social theory can hope to do in this area is identify the potential revolutionary agents. In advanced capitalism the group of people likely to work for more than a reform that leaves systemic structures untouched is,

> that class of people which, by virtue of its function and position in society, is in vital need and is capable of risking what they have and what they can get within the established system in order to replace this system -- a radical change that would involve destruction, abolition of the existing system.[217]

As mentioned above, the people most likely to engage in revolutionary activity are those at the margins, those not already fully integrated into the existing order. For Marcuse this meant students, 'Third World' liberation movements, the civil rights movement, and the women's movement, among others. These people are willing to risk what the system holds in store for them because it is so very little.

Another role of critical social theory is articulating an utopian moment. One of the strongest forces for social integration in late capitalism is the 'necessity of being practical'. This is particularly so among those most well integrated into the system. " Being practical" just means living within the boundaries set by the system. In this situation only utopian thinking can provide a determinate negation of the existing order.

Marcuse argues that through our spontaneous and creative activity (elements of art, revolution and, potentially, everyday life) we construct ourselves, and our relations to the world and other people. Only spontaneous creative activity can break out of the one-dimensionality of life under late capitalism. Utopian thinking, or the "aesthetic dimension," assists our imagination of alternative futures, in part by estranging us from the sheer immediacy of the present.[218] Our utopian imaginings include imagining alternative needs and satisfactions. Remembrance informs us that history moves since the past was different than the present. By remembering the reality of historical change and projecting possible futures that are radically unlike the present, we affirm the possibility of revolution.

We do this in spite of acknowledging the apparent truth of Marcuse's claim that,

> [a] vicious circle seems indeed the proper image of a society which is self-expanding and self- perpetuating in its own preestablished direction -- driven by the growing needs it generates and, at the same time, contains.[219]

A variety of responses to Marcuse's account of the possibilities for radical social change in late capitalism are appropriate at this point. First, in his critique of commodity culture, Marcuse opens himself up to charges of elitism. Charges made all the more forceful by his claim that a socialist state needs "a recognized...elite."[220] Furthermore, a total critique of consumption no longer seems to have much political resonance. As Stanley Aronowitz, among others, has pointed out, the revolutions in former 'Second World' countries have in part been revolutions demanding more commodities and more possibility to consume.[221]

Next, Marcuse seems guilty of fetishizing a romanticized notion of oppositional aesthetic experience. This has two problems. The first problem with Marcuse's notion of the aesthetic is that his account ignores the oppositional practices present in the everyday life of even many of those people most bound to the system. Marcuse seems to ignore both the contradictory moments in and aesthetic possibilities of everyday life, even everyday life in a one-dimensional society.[222] Second, as Marcuse notes:

> The 'end of art' is conceivable only if men are no longer capable of distinguishing between true and false, good and evil, beautiful and ugly, present and future. This would be the state of perfect barbarism at the height of civilization -- and such a state is indeed a historical possibility.[223]

In this passage Marcuse suggests that the assimilative forces of capitalism might be so great as to merge the aesthetic dimension with existing reality. This seems especially true in a time when the culture of consumption (the consumption of culture) has not abated, but has continued throughout the past decade as a major force of social integration.[224]

In the next two chapters I will discuss the efforts of Jürgen Habermas to address some of the lingering questions of the Critical Theory tradition. As I will explain, Habermas suggests a model of rational democratic deliberation on needs and social policy. His theory neither requires any standpoint outside the system, nor does it require a complete and total refusal of participation within the system. For this reason, Habermas' version of Critical Theory is more attentive to the very real gains made even by 'reformist' social movements than is the work of Adorno and Horkheimer. His attempts to re-imagine the crisis points and potential forces of change in late capitalism lead Habermas, like Marcuse, to start with existing oppositional movements. In Chapters V-VII, I will argue that Habermas is, at best, partially successful in his attempt to reconstruct a critical social theory.

# CHAPTER III

# HABERMAS' INITIAL REFORMULATION OF CRITICAL THEORY

> I consider to be false the prognosis that people's anger will . . . evaporate. The anger is structurally generated.[225]

Habermas' early project was to reconstruct the foundations of the Western Marxist tradition as a whole. Part of this project, and what continues to be part of his project, is to rearticulate the liberatory potential of the Enlightenment. As such, his work had as its goal aiding people in their struggles for self-liberation, as it still does today. Though, like the Frankfurt School, Habermas draws on a wide range of disciplines and theoretical approaches, his early work is primarily concerned with developing a solid epistemological foundation for Critical Theory.

In his revision of Critical Theory, Habermas, like the theorists discussed in Chapters I and II, is especially concerned with the role of consciousness in affecting radical social change. Thus, his attempt to provide epistemic justification for Critical Theory includes accounts of the role of instrumental reason, the types of knowledge and their necessary preconditions, and the changing character of the lifeworld. In this reconstructed Critical Theory "critique must recapture its links with the concept of crisis, and in so doing, uncover the yet unresolved crisis of late capitalism."[226] By once again identifying social crisis tendencies, Critical Theory reopens the space for articulating a positive alternative to the present situation and can avoid losing itself in the inescapable mire of a totalized pessimistic critique of everything existing.

## Reconstructing Critical Theory:
## The Return to Marx

> Due to the increasing self-mediation of organized capitalism by means of political intervention and conventions, the structure of economic compulsion can no longer be construed as a closed system.[227]

In his early writings Habermas argues that if a Critical Theory is to retain its practical intent, then it requires a theory of history that justifies confidence in, what might be called, 'human progress' or 'the further development of human liberation'. Habermas argues that Critical Theory as immanent critique can lead to a radical, and ultimately pessimistic, relativism. If no directionality is possible, if we cannot, in principle, distinguish true from false, good from bad, better from worse, then how are we to distinguish between alternatives for acting and living?

If, however, a critical theory can appeal to a theory of history that can distinguish between "what men and things could be and what they actually are,"[228] then immanent critique can retain its practical critical content. As we have already noted, the early work of the Frankfurt School appealed to Marx's theory of history. For this reason, when Habermas began to reconstruct a Critical Theory for the changing conditions of advanced capitalism he first returned to Marx with the aim of reconstructing Marxism. By reconstruction Habermas means the process of "taking a theory apart and putting it back together again in a new form in order to attain more fully the goal it has set for itself."[229]

Habermas argued that advanced capitalist society, what he calls 'modern society', can be characterized by "four historical facts...[which] form an insuperable barrier to any theoretical acceptance of Marxism."[230] These "four facts" are:

1) Advanced capitalism requires political mediation of the sphere of production. This means the state and the economy are inextricably entwined and Marx's model of base/superstructure relation is no longer an accurate model of society. Or, it at least means that Marx's model is not sufficiently subtle and complicated.

2) Because of the rise of the standard of living in advanced capitalist countries, human liberation can no longer be conceived of in purely economic terms. Habermas describes the new conditions as follows:

> The pauperism of alienated labor finds its remote reflection in a poverty of alienated leisure--scurvy and rickets are preserved today in the form of psychosomatic disturbances, hunger and drudgery in the wasteland of externally manipulated motivation, in the satisfaction of needs which are no longer "one's own".[231]

What has happened, in the transition from liberal 'free market' capitalism to advanced capitalism, is the transformation of alienation and domination. Domination, he argues, is no longer directly expressed in wage relations but has come to be embodied in social life itself. This process has been so successful that "those forced to obey, now well integrated, are allowed to do, in the consciousness of their freedom, what do they must."[232]

3) In advanced capitalist society, which can be characterized by the two above conditions, "the proletariat as proletariat, has been dissolved."[233] Like Horkheimer and Adorno, at least in their later work, Habermas finding no revolutionary class-consciousness no longer identifies the working class as potential revolutionary subjects.

4) Marxism in the Soviet Union has come to function as a theory of legitimation for a form of bureaucratic state capitalism and has now been "proven false."

On the basis of these facts, Habermas argues that Marx's theory of history, as originally formulated, is not an adequate ground for a critical social theory with practical intent. What is needed, yet again, is a reconstruction of Marxism that takes account of the new conditions of life under advanced capitalism.

The early Frankfurt School's reconstruction of Marxism had utilized a method of immanent critique. As I have noted above, if the theory of history that underlies the method falls away, then the practical political content of the critique falls away as well. Thus, as the Critical Theorists lived through the transformations to advanced capitalism their theory became a method of total critique directed at the totality of Western reason. Such a critique is theoretically unsatisfactory because it employs the very structures of reason it identifies as oppressive. It is also politically bereft because it no longer claims to be a possible force in material history. Such theory claims to be capable neither of motivating people nor of locating any potential subjects to be motivated. So, critical theory as total critique and total negation is both theoretically and practically problematic, at least it is to a person such as Habermas whose project is one of reconstructing social theory as a critical theory with practical intent.

Continuing the search in Marx's work for a basis for a critical social theory, Habermas examines a tension in Marx's theory -- a tension I have identified as the social being/consciousness relation. As I've noted, Marx's explanation of the relation between social being and consciousness is theoretically and practically unsatisfactory. One reason is that Marx often identifies the self-realization of human beings with the labor process alone. And while it seems likely, given the expressed intent of his work, that he is doing so in order to show both exactly how capital conceives of human beings and how humans in fact come to understand their lives under capitalism; nonetheless, this identification leads to a reduction of the practical concerns of human beings to technical problems. "Because of this," Habermas writes, "Marx's brilliant insight into the dialectical relationship between the forces of production and the relations of production could very quickly be misinterpreted in a mechanistic manner."[234] The result of this is that Marx i) tends toward the claim that continued technical progress will by itself lead to human liberation[235] and ii) cannot explain how it is that humans can become conscious agents of social change.[236] The first outcome leads subsequent Marxist theory in the direction of a deterministic 'orthodox' Marxism and toward its use as a science of legitimation to justify 'necessary' acts which advance history according to the predetermined path outlined by the science of Marxism.[237] The second problem is precisely that which led Horkheimer and Adorno to their pessimism about both technology and revolution because technology came to be equated with domination and was so pervasive that widespread revolutionary consciousness was not possible.

The reduction of the practical to the technical is a condition of modern thought in general. Technocratic consciousness serves to justify particular class interests. But, Habermas argues, it does more than that, technocratic consciousness alters the very structure of the life-world and the nature of human 'self-understanding' and violates our practical interest in 'mutual understanding'.

> Technocratic consciousness makes this practical interest disappear behind the interest in the expansion of our power of technical control.

Thus the reflection that the new ideology calls for must penetrate beyond the level of particular class interests to disclose the fundamental interests of mankind as such, engaged in the process of self-constitution.[238]

Habermas is arguing that the new situation requires a new kind of theory in order to develop a critical perspective on society that retains a practical liberatory intent.[239]

## The Theory of Human Interests: Labor and Interaction

The analysis of the connection of knowledge and interest should support the assertion that a radical critique of knowledge is possible only as social theory.[240]

One of the central contentions of the Frankfurt School, following Lukacs, is that economic crisis alone is not a sufficient condition to bring about radical social change. In order for social change to take place, the conscious efforts of human beings are required. One precondition of humans achieving revolutionary consciousness is the ability to critically understand and evaluate our situation. The ability of a person to critically reflect on the conditions of her or his life is an essential part of liberatory practice. Habermas argues that it is for this reason any account of the everyday life that remains caught in the hermenuetic circle of interpretation and description will be unable to provide the critique and analysis necessary for revolutionary consciousness.

One of the effects of reducing practical concerns to technical questions is to suggest that self-reflection is unnecessary to solve problems; all that is necessary is the right technique. In this way technocratic consciousness obscures the subject and the role of self-reflection in social change. Habermas reaffirms the role of consciousness in liberatory human practice by developing a theory of human interests and their relationship to knowledge and action.[241] Following the tradition we have been tracing from Hegel, Habermas contends that human self-formation, both collective and individual, is a historical process that is realized in social practice. This means that knowledge, as an activity of reflective and historically conditioned subjects, is bound up in human interests. His theory of cognitive interests is intended to explain the relationship of interests and activity. As such, it is a theory of the possibilities of knowledge. Combining the Kantian insight that knowledge is constituted by human subjects with the Hegelian and Marxist claim that human subjectivity is historically and socially conditioned, Habermas understands knowledge to be the result of human attempts to overcome problems they encounter in the process of producing and reproducing everyday life.[242]

Habermas argues in *Knowledge and Human Interests* that human beings have certain interests in terms of which we organize our experience. Though these interests arise from the material history of the human species, they function **a priori** to structure the very possibility of knowledge. Habermas explains:

> They have a transcendental function but arise from actual structures of human life: from structures of a species that reproduces its life through learning processes of socially organized labor and processes of mutual understanding in interaction through mediated language.[243]

Habermas characterizes these interests as "quasi-transcendental" because as **a priori** interests they function as transcendental structures, yet they are formed in the contingent history of the species. The argument that claims to freedom underlie knowledge is a variation of a position also maintained by Kant, Fichte and Hegel. Reason desires that it be free and freedom rests upon self-knowledge. As Hegel argues, no unfree situation can be reasonable. Habermas argues that we have a transcendent interest in human emancipation; the specific content of this interest will be historically variable. That is, what 'freedom' means will be understood within the terms of the existing culture. In this manner, Habermas' theory is a revision of the Critical Theory model of immanent critique.

We are, Habermas notes, both tool using and language using animals. We must produce tools and techniques in order that we can survive our confrontations with nature; we must develop the ability to produce and control objects. As social beings, we must also communicate with each other. Habermas argues that from these two interests, the interest in knowledge that allows the control of objects and the interest in knowledge that allows for communication, follows a third interest. This third interest is in answer to the demand to understand the interest bound nature of all knowledge and demands the self-reflective appropriation of human life. This third interest demands that we submit our lives to rational evaluation. By following this demand we increase our capacity for self-awareness and self-determination (autonomy). In other words, the third interest is an emancipatory interest.

We can now summarize Habermas' first step in reconstructing a critical social theory that affirms the role of consciousness in social change. At this point in the analysis, Habermas has presented the following model of the way in which human beings constitute reality: Human beings have three cognitive interests: technical (tool production and manipulation), practical (communication), and emancipatory. These interests unfold in social life through three social media (means of social organization): labor, interaction and power (relations of dependency and control).[244] Through these media, human cognitive interests give rise to the conditions of three sciences: the empirical-analytic, the historical-hermeneutic and the critical.[245]

As we noted above, Habermas claims the conflation of self-reflection with labor leads to a social theory without emancipatory content. The tendency to engage in this reduction exists not only in bourgeois theorists, but in Marx's work as well: "Marx deludes himself about the nature of reflection when he reduces it to labor."[246] In order to understand exactly why this is the case and why the paradigm of production alone is too narrow a base for critical social theory, I will now turn to a closer examination of Habermas model of human interests.

When Horkheimer argued for a critical social theory he invoked a distinction between traditional and critical theory. Habermas replaced this distinction with a division based on his model of human interests: natural (or empirico-analytic) science, cultural (or historico-hermeneutic) science, and critical science.

The natural sciences are those oriented toward producing technically useful knowledge. Theories in empirico-analytic science aim at predictive knowledge, and are supposed to be value free and grounded in facts themselves. That is, "they grasp reality with regard to technical control that, under specified conditions, is possible everywhere and all times."[247] But, the rules by which we evaluate predictions and by which we determine the relevance of facts to our investigation "are first constituted through an a priori organization of our experience."[248] Taking up the Frankfurt School critique of positivism, Habermas argues that positivist philosophy limits reason's domain to that which can be discovered/created by employing the scientific method. By limiting rationality to technical rationality and declaring all values to be radically subjective (or, at least beyond the realm of rational decidability), positivism is presented with three problems in its self-justification.

First, by claiming all knowledge can be accessed through a single scientific method, positivism must assume, as another of the second generation of critical theorists Karl-Otto Apel has noted, "objective knowledge is possible without intersubjective understanding through communication being presupposed."[249]

Second, by declaring all that is not justifiable by technical rationality to be irrational, positivism marks the realm of practice as beyond rational justification. This means that positivism's commitment in practice to scientific and technological solutions is itself beyond rational justification. Furthermore, practical orientation in life can be ruled out by appeal to reason. As Thomas McCarthy has pointed out, "The cost of abandoning a more comprehensive, substantial concept of reason is an irrational decisionism in the domain of practice."[250]

Finally, positivism can question and explain neither the social preconditions of its own existence, nor its own internal social relations.[251]

Habermas' critique of positivism is not intended to be an argument against natural science as such. Rather he hopes i) to show that technical rationality (instrumental reason) contains and generates values, ii) to thus open up space for discussion of the cultural and critical sciences, and iii) to explore the relations between the natural, cultural and critical sciences.[252]

He writes in part out of the belief that technical knowledge (empirical-analytical science) cannot answer questions about goals and purposes, but that in the modern world many practical questions have been reduced to technical questions. So, often we do not consider whether something ought to happen, we only consider the most effective ways to bring it about. For example: we might not discuss whether train is more efficient than truck transportation, which is a better use of limited resources, and which is better for the long term environmental health of the planet. Instead, we might discuss how to make long haul trucking more efficient - triple trailers, more superhighways, and so on. Admittedly this is sketchy, many details need to be filled in, but the idea is that science and technology do represent, result from some human interests. These are our interests in understanding and controlling our (natural and human made) environment. So, given some goal, S&T can tell us the most efficient means of accomplishing that goal, but often cannot discuss the virtues of the goal itself. Or, given the way things are, S&T can tell us how to accomplish something, but may not be able to tell us if this is how things ought to be.

Science claims to deal with facts, to provide objective knowledge. But, Habermas notes, real science exists as a social enterprise. As such, science is affected by existing social relations. Some sciences can describe these social relations, but by aiming at 'objectivity' these sciences preclude the possibility of evaluating existing social relations. Or, in other words, science cannot explain and evaluate the social preconditions of its own existence. Habermas also argues that science cannot examine its internal social relations - it can tell us the most effective treatments for a disease and the most effective way to build instruments of mass destruction, but **as science**, so long as it pretends to objectivity, cannot evaluate the value of these projects, nor can it explain its tendencies toward "good old boy" networks, response to economic pressures, resistance to new work (especially work which questions the existing presuppositions or social practices of science - for example much research on education suggests that women are discouraged from pursuing scientific careers throughout their time in school. The discouragements range from subtle discouragement of an interest in science to general social attitudes about what sorts of activities are appropriate for girls and boys to support and encouragement from faculty members [studies show that male graduate students in most disciplines receive more positive feedback, more constructive criticism, more personal encouragement and more financial support than do women).

Now, when Habermas claims that science cannot examine i) its social preconditions and ii) its internal social relations, he means that as an expression of technical interests committed to avoiding value judgments science cannot explain these phenomena, though it may be able to describe them. But, science is committed to truth-telling. The goal of an accurate description and explanation of the world requires an interest in open and free communication. If we are interested in controlling (or simply understanding) the world, then we need an accurate model. In order to ensure we have the best possible model, we must test it, examine how it fits with existing models, explore the questions it opens up. Doing so requires that the testing and discussion of theories must aim at truth, at the best possible explanation. To ensure this, science has an interest in openness. In so far as the existing social relations limit open debate, research and testing, then science has an interest in changing those social relations. Out of the actual conditions under which science is practiced, because they fall far short of the ideal and can distort the practice of science, we find that science (and scientists) have an emancipatory interest. If science believes in its own values, then it is committed to allowing the practice of science to proceed with knowledge of why and how some projects are undertaken and others are not.

In contrast to the empirical-analytic sciences, the historical-hermeneutic sciences do not make claims to knowledge that is applicable in all times and places. Rather, "they grasp interpretations of reality with regard to possible intersubjectivity of action-orienting mutual understanding specific to a given hermeneutic starting point."[253] Habermas is not claiming that the cultural sciences describe a different world from that described by the natural sciences. As he writes, they do not "disclose reality under a different transcendental framework."[254] Rather, the cultural sciences are concerned to examine the forms of human interaction and the constructions of meaning on which the natural sciences rest. These forms and constructions are followed beyond the realm of the natural sciences into the whole of the cultural life-world. Habermas clarifies, "The system of the sciences is **one** element of a comprehensive life context, and the latter is the object of the cultural sciences."[255]

Following Dilthey's account of the cultural sciences, Habermas argues that the meaning of social objects and the meanings of the actions are objective in so far as they have a structure that is publicly accessible.

> Meanings, which must always be fixed in symbols, are never private in a rigorous sense. They always have intersubjective validity. Thus, nothing like significance [meaning] could ever constitute itself in a monadically conceived life history. Obviously an expression of life owes its semantic content as much to its place in a linguistic system valid for other subjects as it does to its place in a biographical context.[256]

Meanings, Habermas is arguing, are never simply private, nor are they just the product of linguistic communication. Rather, life-histories are constituted by the experiences of individual subjects over time **and** the intersubjective mutual communication with others. At this intersection, the intersection of the diachronic dimension of individual histories and the synchronic dimension of communication with others, self-consciousness constitutes itself and meanings are constructed. The goal of the cultural sciences is to explicate these meanings.

The interest of the cultural sciences is to further mutual understanding. "The understanding of meaning is directed in its very structure toward the attainment of possible consensus among actors in the framework of a self understanding derived from consensus."[257] Since the cultural sciences seek to understand meaning, and since meaning is constituted through mutual understanding of self and other, the cultural sciences have a practical interest in overcoming conflicts of interpretation and misunderstandings.

Habermas notes that both the natural and the cultural sciences aim at nomological knowledge. However, a critical social science involves reflection on the structures under investigation, reflection on when the theory grasps regularities of social action and reflection on when theory has served the ideological function of describing existing social conditions which could be otherwise (i.e.: social conditions which are historically contingent) as such ahistorical regularities. "Thus the level of unreflected consciousness, which is one of the initial conditions of such laws, can be transformed."[258]

Habermas contends that the most sophisticated forms of historical-hermeneutic science, Dilthey's and Gadamer's hermeneutics, fail as critical social theories. The reason they fail is, as it was for the empirical-analytic sciences, the failure of critical reflection of their own conditions of existence. Dilthey's hermeneutics is one of description and demands an objective observer who suspends critical judgment. This approach assumes that the hermeneutic process affects neither the interpreter nor that which is interpreted. Meaning is whatever the subjects of study say it is, and the interpreter is able to have ready access to these meanings.

> It appears as though the interpreter transposes himself into the horizon of the world or language from which a text derives its meaning....Just as positivist self-understanding does not take into account explicitly the connection between measurement operations and feedback control, so it eliminates from consideration the interpreter's pre-understanding. Hermeneutic knowledge is always mediated through this pre-

understanding, which is derived from the interpreter's initial situation.[259]

Habermas is arguing that historicism, such as Dilthey's, in the cultural sciences plays the same role as positivism in the natural sciences, it blocks examination of the preconditions of the science. In the case of the cultural sciences the notion of interest free observation blocks one of the central insights of hermeneutics: that the cultural scientist is also embedded in history and that s/he cannot escape her or his own language or life history. Thus, a cultural science following Dilthey's model will twice fail to be critical as it will i) block critical evaluation of a given object of study in favor of description and ii) will block examination of the preconditions of the description (i.e.: the interpreter's life-history).

Habermas understands Gadamer's hermeneutics to be a significant advance over Dilthey's in so far as Gadamer argues that understanding is realized in language and that as the form of human intersubjectivity language is constitutive of human life.[260] Attempts at *Verstehen* involve the interpreter's attempt to explain in her or his own language meanings that arise in another linguistic context. The process requires an initial interpretation that is revised through further research and reflection, including research and reflection into the interpreter's own history and expectations. The two parties, interpreter and interpreted, enter into a dialogue with a whole set of beliefs, expectation and practices which are the product of tradition. Thus, tradition is an integral part of the hermeneutic process, and in so far as tradition is historically constituted then i) there can be no final interpretation, and ii) the hermeneutic process itself will contribute to our self-understanding (i.e.: our traditions will be subject to pressures to change as they encounter other traditions).

Habermas agrees with Gadamer on a substantial number of issues: cultural scientists cannot escape their own socio-historical context; understanding is context dependent; our interpretive interactions with others are important for self-understanding. But, Gadamer is too quick to accept tradition and its underlying consensus. An uncritical acceptance of tradition fails to recognize that consensus may be coerced. As Habermas notes, "every consensus, in which the understanding of meaning terminates, stands fundamentally under suspicion of being pseudo-communicatively induced."[261] Gadamer does not take sufficient account of the extent to which tradition and language are dependent upon other social products and can function to conceal underlying conditions of social life, conditions of domination and repression. In other words, to invoke the language of the Hegelian-Marxist tradition, Gadamer is too enamored of appearance and not sufficiently aware of the reified nature of appearance.[262]

In order to understand the nature and possibilities of social action, a critical social theory is necessary, a theory which takes account of both labor and linguistic interaction. Such a theory will provide an analysis of the unacknowledged conditions that often block human self-realization. The demand for critical theory arises from the human interest in emancipation that is based in the human capacity to be self-constituting, self-reflective, rational creatures. Such capacities are, Habermas argues, blocked not only by the cultural conditions of advanced capitalism in general, but also by the knowledge conditions characteristic of the natural and cultural sciences. In order to allow the process of human self-formation to occur under conditions free from unacknowledged constraints, a form of knowledge adequate to identifying and abolishing such constraints is necessary. Habermas identifies this type of knowledge as that gained through a process of self-reflection.

> Self-reflection brings to consciousness those determinates of a self-formative process of cultivation and self-formation which ideologically determine a contemporary practice and conception of the world...[Self-reflection] leads to insight due to the fact that what has previously been unconscious is made conscious in a manner rich in consequences: analytic insights intervene in life.[263]

What is needed is a practice based in self-reflective apprehension of our actual material conditions and the possibilities they offer for human emancipation. Such a practice, which will unblock our critical capacities, is what Habermas calls an emancipatory practice. One candidate for an emancipatory practice is Freudian psychoanalysis.

When Habermas turns to Freud as an exemplar of a person engaged in emancipatory activity he is following the lead of earlier Critical Theorists. However, unlike Adorno for whom Freud's work served to justify the non-identity of the social and the psychological,[264] and unlike Marcuse who refashioned Freud into a theory of remembered and potential utopia,[265] Habermas uses Freud as a methodological model. By moving from an emphasis on the content of Freud's theories to an emphasis in the methodology, Habermas believes he has found, in

Freud, a method of personal ideology critique that can serve as a model for a critique of social ideologies.

> Psychoanalysis is relevant to us as the only tangible example of a science incorporating methodological self-reflection. The birth of psychoanalysis opens up the possibility of arriving at the dimension that positivism closed off . . . . This possibility has remained unrealized. For the scientific self-misunderstanding of psychoanalysis inaugurated by Freud himself . . . , sealed off this possibility.[266]

Habermas argues that Freud's work, like that of Marx, is open to a scientistic misunderstanding because of the author's tendency to claim for his work the status of a natural science. What interests Habermas about psychoanalysis is its construction of interpretive frameworks with the goal of aiding the reconstruction of the patient's life history. In this way psychoanalysis differs from hermeneutics. Whereas the hermeneutic sciences aim at a consensually accepted description, a critical science aims at a critical self-reflection that is accepted or rejected based on its ability to overcome certain pathologies in everyday life.[267]

Only through the process of self-reflection are we able to grasp the connection between knowledge and interest. The emancipatory interest arises in response to the pathological distortions of communicative and productive interactions. Freudian psychoanalysis reveals the systematic distortions of communication and action in an individual life. Both the patient and the analyst undertake this process of revelation in order to remove the pathologies from the individual life.

Habermas argues that this model of individual emancipation can be transferred to social theory. This is because "the same configurations that drive individuals to neurosis move society to establish institutions."[268] Habermas' interpretation of Freud holds that social institutions are effective in facilitating survival, but at the cost of repressing needs and wants by distorting communication.

> [J]ust as in the clinical situation, so in society, pathological compulsion is accompanied by the interest in its abolition. Both the pathology of social institutions and that of individual consciousness reside in the medium of language and of communicative action and assume the form of a structural deformation of language.[269]

According to Habermas, Marx was unable to give an adequate account of ideology and power because of his emphasis on the paradigm of production. In reformulating Marx, Habermas uses Freud to develop a critique of the ways in which late capitalism systematically distorts communication. That is, Habermas uses the Freudian insight that "emancipation entails not only overcoming constraints of nature, but also dissolving systems of distorted communication"[270] in order to identify social crisis points.

Habermas has argued that in order to formulate a critical social theory with practical intent we can no longer base our theory solely within the paradigm of production. We must expand our account of the organizing principles of modern society to include communicative interaction. In fact, it is in the systematic distortions of communicative interaction that the new crisis points of capitalism arise. By valorizing the psychoanalyst as the model for a critical social theorist, Habermas has proposed a theory of "the enlightenment's talking cure."[271]

Several problems arise when considering psychoanalysis as a model of emancipatory practice. In psychoanalysis both parties are willing to enter into the dialogue. When we extrapolate from the analyst-patient situation to the level of a social whole two difficulties appear. First, we have no reason to expect the ruling class to willing enter into a dialogue which would likely result in a radical change in their ways of life. History certainly gives us no hope in this regard.[272] Second, psychoanalysis requires someone outside the 'troubled' individual who is trying to expunge the neurosis. At the social level, the social whole is analogous to the individual. No outside position is possible for a social psychoanalyst. Since this is the case, we will be talking to ourselves. Talking to ourselves (to myself, one's self) can be beneficial; however, it is not the same model of emancipatory discourse Habermas identifies in the practice of psychoanalysis.

A further problem arises if we consider psychoanalysis from a Foucauldian perspective. As Habermas notes, and valorizes, psychoanalysis is a practice of reconstructing individuals. In whose interests and toward what ends are individual psyches reconstructed? The goal of psychoanalysis is to allow the individual to survive and function in their everyday life. That is, the goal is to approach 'normalcy'. The analyst-patient relation is similar to many disciplinary relationships (parent-child, teacher-student, husband-wife, clergy, layperson) in that one party has more power within the relationship.

These relationships function to construct certain sorts of people, not to uncover, or emancipate, a 'true' self. The relationship between the analyst and patient is a paradigm case of disciplinary power. This being the case, it is not at all clear that psychoanalysis is an emancipatory practice.[273]

In fairness to Habermas, I think another interpretation of his valorization of psychoanalysis is possible. Perhaps the concrete realization of an emancipatory interest demands equality as a precondition. In the context of my earlier discussion of Hegel's dialectic of Lordship and Bondage I noted that what we desire (require?) from another is recognition. As Hegel argued, in conditions of conflict, and inequality, genuine recognition is impossible. This is so, in part, because each party attempts to construct, to validate, to be independently, alone, over and against the other. In such a situation, psychoanalysis might be a dialogue toward mutual reconstruction -- a dialogue that aims at avoiding the damaging hierarchy of the dialectic of Lordship and Bondage. This process differs from that proposed by Freud in that each person is both analyst and analyzed. I believe something of this sort is at work in Habermas' discussion of the ideal speech situation.[274]

## Legitimation in Modern Society:
## Ideology and Crisis

Thus far in this chapter I have argued that Habermas is interested i) in continuing a self-proclaimed process of theorizing the possibilities of human liberation and ii) in doing so by returning to 'crisis theory'. Not only does he argue for the category of interaction as a necessary addition to labor in any social theory, but he also locates the most likely crisis tendencies in advanced capitalism as occurring in the sphere of interaction. These crises are crises of legitimation. As Habermas argues in *Toward a Rational Society*, "[c]lass antagonisms...have become latent."[275] So, while crises do still occur, economic crises that is, they are masked/hidden from view or appear as something other than the result of crisis in capitalism. However, crises in the 'base' do still occur. Today, the primary crisis points are within the realm of interaction.

Early in the 1960s Habermas documents these four trends of twentieth century life: 1) the growth of large scale economic and commercial organizations, 2) the growing interdependence of science, technology and industry, 3) the growing interdependence of the state, economy and society, 4) the continued extension of instrumental reason.[276] The result of these trends is that "politics is no longer only a phenomenon of the superstructure."[277]

Habermas finds it necessary to rewrite Marx, especially Marxian crisis theory because the changes in the organization of capitalism, the ideological belief that science and technology will solve human problems, and the increased integration of the state and the economy, have lead to the reduction of practical and political questions to technical questions. The reduction of the political to the technical has lead to a depoliticization of society. Now we have the aforementioned ideological faith in the power of technology. This ideology is more pervasive and harder to oppose than traditional 'political' ideologies. The belief in technicity becomes written into everyday practice and suppresses alternatives in the name of economy and efficiency. In such a situation we seldom debate ends. We only debate means, and then in terms of which is most 'practical' or 'efficient'.[278]

In the 19th century Marx debunked the ideology of a 'free' exchange in the market place. As we have discussed, economic analysis alone will not suffice to explain the functions of state, economy and society. In *Theory and Practice*, Habermas argues that we need an analysis of both the legitimation of the state and the cultural forces which support the state. This is necessary, in part, because the character of capitalism and capitalist oppression has changed since Marx wrote. Habermas notes: i) that oppression is increasingly psychological and ethical, ii) that oppression is no longer economic,[279] and iii) that the proletariat no longer constitutes a potentially revolutionary force.

As a result of capitalism's success at managing economic crisis, Habermas turns, in *Legitimation Crisis* (first published in German in 1973), to the spheres of legitimation and motivation in order to locate likely sites for systemic crisis in late capitalism. His primary question is: "[I]n what crisis tendency does the temporarily suppressed, but unresolved class antagonism express itself?"[280]

Habermas identifies three types of crisis in late capitalism: i) economic, ii) political, or a crisis of rationality, and iii) socio-cultural, or crises of legitimation and motivation. According to Habermas, managing a crisis at one of these levels leads to its reappearance on another level. Following Habermas, I will discuss first economic crisis, then political crisis, and, finally, legitimation crisis.

As the history of capitalism has shown, economic crisis is not inevitable. Economic crises can arise from i) the internal logic of capitalism that includes, ii) conflict between workers and capitalists. One way to avoid economic crisis is through state intervention in the economy. In the twentieth century, long periods of 'steady economic growth' have been achieved by state mediation of class conflict. A compromise between labor and capital is overseen by a supposedly impartial state. This means two things. First, the state will systematically intervene in the economy in order to thwart economic crisis (Keynsianism). Second, the economy no longer appears to be autonomous and "crisis manifestations in advanced capitalism have lost their nature-like character."[281] That is, previous economic crises might appear to be the result of systemic problems in the economy. Economic crises were understood to arise from the 'nature' of the economic order. Because of increased state intervention, economic crises are now understood as crises of management, or political crises.[282]

The steps taken by the state to avert economic crisis create a crisis of rationality. This is so because there **are** conflicts of interest within capitalism. The purpose of state intervention is to mediate between the different conflicting interests in the economy: the interest in allocation of resources and legislation to support economic growth, and the interest in compensating the victims of economic growth. However, these conflicting interests often make contradictory demands upon the state. For this reason the state cannot fully meet the demands of each party. In attempts to partially meet conflicting demands, and at the same time avoid systemic crisis, aid and intervention are not distributed equally, in fact, they tend to be distributed so as to perpetuate existing social relations.[283] A differential distribution of resources that aims at systemic preservation should be no surprise as the state has an interest in its own preservation. But, the tendency of state intervention to consistently favor some interests (i.e.: 'national' over 'special' interests[284]) over others stands in contradiction to the official state function of impartially, and rationality, mediating and managing conflict. State intervention raises questions of interest and control and gives rise to a legitimation crisis.[285]

Habermas rejects the view of state capitalism held by earlier Critical Theorists. On Habermas' account, the state usually acts in the interest of existing economic relations, but sometimes it acts in the interests of those victimized by the status quo. According to his account, if the state did not have to submit its decisions and actions to public debate, then it could easily manage the economy in a 'rational' and 'practical' manner. The problem is sometimes characterized by social critics from the right as the problem of "too much democracy," a thinly veiled version of Plato's fear of the mob. One response to this problem is to structure the political system so as to discourage participation and debate.[286] Another strategy is to construct ideologies that legitimate existing relations as the best possible conditions. Habermas notes that in spite of capitalism's success in constructing happy consumer consciousness and in privatizing (depoliticizing) areas of discourse, demands for state intervention on behalf of better working conditions, healthcare, childcare, AIDS research, differently-abled access, education, and welfare continue.

As I noted above, the state's necessarily partial attempts to meet the contradictory demands placed upon it lead to socio-cultural crises. The apparent indifference of the state, the difficulty of affecting change, the predominance of technical rationality, and the continued growth of consumer culture, all lead to a cynicism about politics. Part of the fallout from this cynicism is the fading of the 'inner necessity' of work, and a growing lack of interest in competition. As those who least benefit from the system increasingly refuse to compete for the scarce resources offered them by the system, we arrive at a motivation crisis.

## The Ideal Speech Situation and the Crisis of Social Integration

One way of thinking about the crises of motivation and legitimation is as crises of social integration. The beliefs that exist in order to facilitate social integration fail to legitimate the existing order and fail to motivate many people to participate. In the early 1970s, when he wrote *Legitimation Crisis*, Habermas argued that these crisis tendencies are gaining momentum and that a systemic crisis appeared likely.

One of the moving forces behind the socio-cultural crises of late capitalism is the emancipatory ideal that is implicit in the acts of speech. Habermas argues that the very act of speech presupposes the possibility of an ideal speech situation where the force of the better argument alone will prevail.[287] Furthermore, the ideal speech situation functions as a regulative ideal against which we can compare our existing society.[288]

Habermas claims that when we speak we wish to achieve an understanding; we wish to communicate with each other. For this reason, communicative interaction presupposes four claims about its own practice. When I speak I assume: 1) that what I say is comprehensible, 2) that what I say is true, 3) that what I say is appropriate to this context, 4) that what I say is sincerely meant.[289] These assumptions underlay every speech situation; however, they may not be concretely realized in every speech situation. That is, we may intend understanding when we talk; nonetheless, we might not achieve understanding.

Habermas argues that reaching an understanding presupposes that we can genuinely understand each other, and that it is possible to distinguish between a genuine understanding and a deceptive understanding. According to Habermas, a genuine understanding is based solely on the force of the better argument. If we agree, our agreement should not be based upon any hidden factors or prior constraints on speech. If we reach a genuine understanding, it is based on the force of the better argument alone. This can only be the case if all possible participants (i.e.: all affected parties) have an equal opportunity to freely participate in the debate.[290] In this way we arrive at the 'ideal speech situation', a situation of discursive practice much like Kant's 'Kingdom of Ends'.[291]

In order to achieve a genuine understanding at the social level, all members of a society must have an equal opportunity to participate. For this reason we must change our society in order to ensure that discussion, communication, and opinion formation is free from coercive control and manipulation. In this way, implicit in beginning to speak is an interest in the ideal speech situation. In making this argument, Habermas is attempting to ground a human emancipatory interest in the universal, for humans, condition of communicating with each other.

In his argument for the implicit character of the ideal speech situation, Habermas is making the assumption common to philosophers that if a rational argument is laid out, then people will agree and respond accordingly. It seems to me that this argument is highly problematic.

First, it does not follow from the fact that a person understands an argument that s/he will necessarily agree with it. For example, during the mid-late 1980s, a person could have watched a television newscast about the 'October Surprise,'[292] or Iran-Contra, or US backed and trained death squads in Central America and understood that some actions undertaken by the then president (or vice-president) of the U.S.

were perhaps illegal and that he had violated his oath of office. At the same time, one need not agree with the conclusion that the president should be impeached.

This seemingly unreasonable situation might make more sense if we consider the fact that a genuine agreement is seldom based on the force of better argument alone. More often than not, understandings and agreements involve personal allegiances, preconceptions, prejudices, sympathies, political projects, or love.[293]

The important qualifier in Habermas' theory is the claim that the force of the better argument will prevail only when communication is free from hidden constraints. From this caveat follows the practical implications of his account of the ideal speech situation. One possible explanation of the above 'problems' with Habermas' theory is that we do not now even come close to the ideal speech situation.

Habermas understands that power relations distort communication. In *Legitimation Crisis*, he argues that resistance to hidden constraints was increasing and that bourgeois consciousness seemed to be entering a period of disintegration.[294] He projected a looming legitimation crisis in capitalism when the contradiction between existing class structures and the democratic values implicit in speaking would become increasingly clear to more and more people. The very act of speech itself demands discourse conditions that stand in direct opposition to the present class compromise.

However, the looming crisis has not occurred. A central part of the politics of the last 20 years has been to reinvigorate the work ethic, reemphasize possessive individualism, remilitarize (increasingly against ourselves), encourage increasing consumerism, and now, in the early 1990s, reinvent faith in 'American' technology and ability to act effectively and unilaterally in the world.

Against this backdrop we now turn to Habermas' theory of the colonization of the lifeworld. As we shall see, the colonization theory presented in *The Theory of Communicative Action* updates the crisis theory developed in *Legitimation Crisis*. The new formulation does not rest upon an implicit ideal speech situation, and it locates more social pathologies and more potential crisis points.

# CHAPTER IV

## THE COLONIZATION OF THE LIFEWORLD

### System and Lifeworld

> Members of a collective normally share a life-world. In communication, but also in the process of cognition, this only exists in the distinctive, pre-reflexive form of background assumptions, background receptives, or background relations. The lifeworld is that remarkable thing which dissolves and disappears before our eyes as soon as we try to take it up piece by piece.[295]

During the course of his intellectual production Habermas has moved from a version of ideology critique to a criticism of social reification. Or, from an attempt to provide a grounding of a critical social theory in "quasi-transcendental" structures of human interests to an account of the colonization of a linguistically based lifeworld by an instrumentally oriented social system through the media of power and money. In making this move Habermas is paralleling moves in Anglo-American and French philosophy from the paradigm of consciousness to the paradigm of language.[296]

A primary motivation for this move is the growing critique of the philosophy of consciousness with its origin in the works of Freud, Heidegger and Nietzsche. Part of the critique of the philosophy of consciousness is a rejection of the project of the Enlightenment,[297] a claim that the Enlightenment project with its privileging of abstract rationality and individual autonomy is inextricably entwined with modern forms of domination.

As mentioned in preceding chapters, the Kantian, Hegelian and Marxian projects can be situated within a historical period we can call modernism (roughly the time since the Enlightenment). Each conceptualized the modern (or Enlightenment) as a process of social and cultural differentiation moved by and revolving around developmental logics located within the differentiating value and action spheres. Modernity is a series of separate developmental logics including the logic of democracy, the logic of capitalism and the logic of industrialization.[298] Tendencies that characterize modernity are the capitalization of social life, the conception of persons as autonomous, industrialization, the autonomization of art, the democratization of debates about civil society and the state. Conflict within society occurs because of the clash between i) the development of the public sphere (associated with democracy and autonomy) and ii) the tendency of the state to absorb society (associated industrialization and the rise of capitalism).[299]

Habermas' goal, especially in *The Theory of Communicative Action*, is to reconstruct the Enlightenment project. Toward that end he offers us a two level theory of society utilizing both lifeworld and social system perspectives and develops a new critical social theory that describes and explains the pathologies of modern society while still retaining the emancipatory content of certain Enlightenment ideals.[300]

On Habermas' account the lifeworld is the unthematized background of meanings against which particular events occur. Habermas integrates three different existing approaches into his account of the lifeworld; i) the phenomenological (Husserl and Schutz) with its emphasis on the production and reproduction of cultural knowledge, ii) the social systems approach (Durkheim, Parsons and Luhmann) with its focus on the role of institutions and social integration, and iii) symbolic interactionism (Mead) with its emphasis on the role of socialization and the lifeworld as a ground for the formation of personality, for individual growth and action. By combining these three theoretical perspectives Habermas arrives at a description of the lifeworld as a preexisting stock of meanings[301] handed down in culture and language. Under conditions of modernity the lifeworld becomes rationalized. That is, the lifeworld possesses linguistic structures that allow the differentiation of objective, social and subjective domains of reference.[302]

Every action includes a complex set of objective facts, social norms, and personal experiences. Depending upon the situation some of these conditions will emerge from and some will fade into the lifeworld. These actions/events are unified into a life history through narratives, through communicative action.[303] Habermas identifies three dimensions of communicative rationality, not surprisingly they correspond to the three domains/viewpoints within the lifeworld. They are: first, the knowing subject and its relation to the world of events; second, the acting practical subject in its relation to a social world; third, the suffering passionate subject in its relation to its own and others subjectivity.[304] It is through these communicatively structured relations that cultural reproduction, the coordination of social interaction, and socialization take place.[305]

Unlike many of his predecessors (Lukacs and Marcuse come to mind), Habermas argues that the rationalization of the lifeworld, its separation into different spheres of knowledge and action, is a positive result of modernity. The rationalized lifeworld allows the structural differentiation of i) culture from society -- this frees normative institutions (such as the courts) from metaphysical or religious worldviews (at least in theory); ii) personality from culture -- this frees individuals to revise traditions, to participate freely in interpersonal relationships, and to engage in self-conscious self-realization; and iii) form from content -- this includes freeing formal procedures of justice from concrete action contexts, and cognitive structures from particular life histories. The rationalized lifeworld also requires greater reflexivity in decision-making. One result of these trends is that specialized disciplines emerge, democratic institutions replace authoritarian institutions, and education "de-parochializes."[306]

Habermas draws on the work of Jean Piaget and Lawrence Kohlberg in order to argue that linguistic evolution and moral-cognitive development parallel social evolution and the rationalization of the lifeworld. At the 'highest' level of moral-cognitive development (the postconventional stage), people can evaluate norms from the standpoint of the generalized other (roughly the perspective of one employing the Kantian Categorical Imperative). Communication at this level requires the ability to debate, propose, and reject value claims from a universal perspective.[307]

This process leads to the possibility of critical learning and discourse when knowledge claims, normative claims, and descriptions of subjective experience can be distinguished from each other in everyday conversation. Finally expert discourses (politics, science, medicine, law, philosophy, ethics, art, and theology) split off from everyday speech.[308] The process of rationalization constructs persons who are increasingly autonomous with respect to culture, tradition, and history. Individuals who demand a greater say in determining the course of their lives. As we shall find, when systemic logics invade the lifeworld people organize resistance movements, what Habermas calls the 'new social movements'.

From the viewpoint internal to the lifeworld "society is represented as a network of communicatively mediated cooperation . . . . The lifeworld that members construct from common cultural traditions is coextensive with society."[309] But such a viewpoint is a mistake. It is a mistake not in that it is false, but because it is only partial.[310] If society is equated with lifeworld, then the source of social pathologies and crises remain enigmatic, and in response to social pathologies we receive such edifying discourses as bourgeois psycho-babble and eco-babble. Furthermore, such an equation requires the acceptance of "three fictions": i) that culture and ordinary language is transparent, ii) that communicative action is characterized by reciprocity and the participants "have to assume that they could, in principle, arrive at an understanding about anything and everything,"[311] and iii) that individuals are fully conscious of their motives.

According to Habermas these fictions are an account of,

> "the way things look to the members of the sociocultural lifeworld themselves. In fact, however, their goal directed actions are coordinated not only through processes of reaching understanding, but also through functional interconnections that are not intended by them, and are usually not even perceived within the horizon of everyday practice."[312]

Habermas is claiming that there are forces external to the lifeworld that are the sources of distortion in the communicative action of the lifeworld, sources of social pathologies. These social pathologies include such symptoms of modern life as anomie, alienation, neurosis, and the loss of meaning, security and identity provided by being firmly situated in a culture.

Habermas agrees with Weber's account of rationalization. As Weber demonstrated alienation and despair do follow demythologization, bureaucratization, and mechanization. Habermas is not willing to stop here, he argues that the loss of freedom and meaning is more than adequately compensated for by the positive and enabling consequences

of rationalization. The positive consequences of rationalization include:
    1) new prospects for freedom and autonomy, the enhancement of individual autonomy with respect to tradition, and
    2) the emergence of new possibilities for meaning in new forms of art, and in increased possibilities for democracy brought about, in part, by new technologies.

The rationalization process becomes pathological because of the one-sided selective institutionalization of rationality that stems from advanced capitalism. This process Habermas calls the "colonization of the lifeworld."

Weber fails to fully account for the dynamics of social pathology because: 1) he conflates capitalism and rational society, 2) he conflates purposive rationality (instrumental or technical reason) with reason itself, and 3) he focuses his sociology on an agents' self-understanding of his or her situation.

According to Habermas, the result of these aspects of Weber's theory lead him to conclude that the process of cultural rationalization is the sole cause of social pathologies. This interpretation completely neglects the unintended consequences that arise from the fact that social systems do not always function rationally.[313] In order to understand the sources of social pathologies we must examine the systems of i) economic organization and ii) political and bureaucratic action.

From the lifeworld point of view society is the coordination of action through communicative interaction. From the system's perspective, society is a self-regulating system. In this system actions are coordinated through the imperatives of means/ends rationality. That is, actions are chosen because of the ways in which their consequences will fit with the consequences of other actions already chosen. From this perspective society is understood in terms of the functional relations of its systems and subsystems as understood from the perspective of an external observer. Of course, neither the system nor the lifeworld perspective is **merely** a perspective. Each viewpoint corresponds to something about society. And, though the lifeworld perspective has a certain priority because it is in principle possible that all functions of actions be expressed in the lifeworld structures of communicative action, the importance of the systems approach has been increasing with the increasing complexity of society.[314]

Habermas argues that both system and lifeworld perspectives must be used to understand contemporary society. Furthermore, in his positive program he argues that each will be a necessary component of future social organizations. I think this can be clarified if we examine what would happen is either system of lifeworld is pushed to its limit and completely occludes the other. A complete lifeworld would be anarchy: no rules, no way to maintain order, no way to organize 'rationally' the complexities of modern society. WE might then be left with something similar to a Hobbesian state of nature. Although he has disavowed his 'fascism of the left' remark about some aspects of the student revolt in the 1960s, something like the sort of fear evidenced in that remark seems to underlay Habermas insistence on retaining systemic rationality and organization in any new society. A society fully absorbed into the system would be fully cybernized. This is the sort of world of total control and manipulation is similar to that found in Huxley's *Brave New World* and most works of Philip K. Dick. This may be the world Baudrillard celebrates (?) in *America*. In such a world the gains of rationalization are wiped out be a triumph of technical rationality.[315]

Following Parsons, Habermas argues that the system and lifeworld are interrelated and looped together in a feedback process. In fact the functions of systemic integration attended to by the system have their origin in the social integration of the lifeworld. The increased rationalization of the lifeworld and the increasing requirements made by the material reproduction of modern society means that the activities of individuals must be increasingly coordinated. In the institutionalization of this coordination an "uncoupling of system and lifeworld" occurs.[316] In order to clarify this process, I will now turn to Habermas account of "power" in modern societies.

## Power and Money as "Steering Media"

As the rationalization of the lifeworld progresses in the transition from traditional to modern societies, there is greater the chance that disagreements will occur. In traditional societies institutions linked to social integration -- such as kinship systems, ritual exchange, and so on

-- served to coordinate power and exchange relations. With the fading of consensus about the meaning of many situations came increasing strain on the social structure.[317] To deal with this pressure certain mechanisms of systemic organization were decoupled from the demands of communicative action.[318]

Through a process that Habermas, borrowing from Parsons, calls "value generalization,"[319] areas of life are transferred from the lifeworld to the system. As society becomes more complex, positions of power are detached from kinship systems and annexed to political office. In these increasingly politically stratified societies a justification of power becomes necessary. And, as we will examine in what follows, power cannot be legitimated in terms of money. After all, the market is supposedly a place of 'free' and 'equal' exchange where everyone makes what he can of, and for, himself, being all he can be, on the basis only of talent and hard work. In such a place, power should be irrelevant. Thus state functions, such as judicial and legislative, become formally organized, codified in a system of formal law. One aspect of these legal arrangements is their guarantee of "free contracts" for private gain. This elevates the market to the status of an autonomous self-regulating system.[320]

In *Legitimation Crisis*, Habermas argues that one of the effects of situating the market as an autonomous sphere within society is to contain class conflict by concealing class exploitation. The transition to bourgeois civil law does maintain law and order, and provide for education, transportation and communication. This transition also leaves the market untouched, largely free from regulation. The market then relieves the political order of the need for legitimation because the conditions of freedom are now found in the market where the exchange of "equivalents" and the "voluntary" nature of wage relations hide exploitation.[321]

Habermas revises this argument in *The Theory of Communicative Action* and introduces the notion of the steering medium. Just as money is the steering medium by which market decisions are coordinated, so to are administrative/political systems integrated through "anonymous forms of system integrative sociation."[322]

In many ways the system/lifeworld distinction serves to reconceive Marx's distinction between base and superstructure. One theoretical and practical result of Marx's distinction was the ability to analyze aspects of society not immediately available to consciousness (Hegel's appearance/reality distinction again). Habermas describes the uncoupling and rationalization of system and lifeworld as aspects of modernity. The lifeworld reproduces itself through the symbolic interactions of people in their everyday lives. The subsystems of the economy and the state reproduce themselves through the media of power and money. The social distortion that Marx sought to explain is explained by Habermas as the process whereby the reproduction of everyday life becomes directed by considerations of money and power and not through the communicative interactions of people. This is the colonization of the lifeworld. The efficient pursuit of goals that we never debated becomes the point of our lives.

Money functions as a steering media through the familiar process of commodification. Money converts concrete labor into an abstract commodity. This process takes place in the exchange relations of the market place. Habermas observes that the exchange relation does not obviously disadvantage any participants, because no party will enter into an exchange relation that is not in her own interest. For this reason, the market appears to be an autonomous sphere of non-normative activity. Power is the medium whereby individual decisions are coordinated toward "the realization of collective goals." It is through the medium of power that the actions of administrative-bureaucratic structures come to appear as the nature-like relations that defined Weber's iron cage. But, Habermas claims, unlike exchange relations, the power relation is not obviously in the interest of all parties. Thus, the power relation "needs to be legitimated and therefore calls for a more demanding normative anchoring than money."[323]

Habermas is arguing that although power functions as a steering medium, just as money does, it still requires justification in communicative terms. This is so because of the structure of power relations. Powerholders have an advantage over subordinates. Habermas makes this claim based, in part, upon Luhmann's account in *The Differentiation of Society*. Luhmann argues that power is the medium by which modern societies reduce the complexity of decision-making. Decisions made by powerholders become the unquestioned basis of decisions by subordinates.[324]

In this account of the structure of power relations in modern society, Habermas may be correct. Yet, it seems quite possible that power has disappeared into the fabric of the system, and the system-lifeworld interaction, just as money has. If this has happened, than power will no more need justification than does money because it (power) will no longer appear as such. In fact, we need only remember the new ideology of business (or government) that "we're all in this together" in order to find reason to doubt that his analysis is complete. As evidence of this we find workers' quality circles, public hearings, citizens' committees, and the construction of a singular 'us' to be counterposed to an external enemy such as communism, terrorism, or drugs. All of these devices function to remove political considerations and power relations from the administrative decision process by supposedly including all interested parties in the process. The effect is to remove, or to appear to have removed, hierarchy from the decision making process.[325]

Habermas is aware of these possibilities. In his discussion of value generalization he identifies two of its potential negative effects. First, the goal of a rationalized lifeworld is the increasingly universal character of our normative judgments and a growth in the spheres governed by consensus-oriented communication. But, consensus oriented communication is difficult because we are not always able to confront the other interested parties, nor are we always able to completely justify all assumptions underlying our conduct. Second, communication might not move us towards consensus but instead make clear disagreements that would otherwise be unnoticed.[326] The process of value generalization thus increases the possibility of dissent and conflict and provides conditions when power might have to be made obvious in order to maintain social control.

However, the danger of dissent is blunted by the very same process of rationalization and value generalization through strategic and consensually motivated actions. First, the possibility of conflict is thwarted by appealing to the values of efficiency and success. In the move to success-oriented action authority and prestige (power) and influence (the resources at one's disposal, or money) are used to strategically motivate action.[327] This move gives a motivation and goal to action that both provides justification for conduct and allows disagreements among the involved parties to remain hidden. The same is true for the move to consensually motivated action. By condensing consensual communication, authority and prestige (here manifest as reliability and reputation), and influence (here the resources are knowledge and information) serve to rationally justify action. Thus not only are disagreements kept hidden, but the need to confront the other involved parties is removed because all involved have agreed to allow certain aspects of communication to be condensed.[328]

The mass media facilitate the process of condensing communicative action. They do so by promoting the conditions where i) a class of specialists and ii) hierarchies of knowledge and authority can exist.[329] These conditions relieve us of the need to confront certain areas of the lifeworld. This is good in so far as the consensual condensation of communication aids in our generating both consensus in complex societies and a public sphere.[330]

Thus we find that Habermas' own account of the processes of rationalization of the lifeworld and value generalization give us reasons to believe that both steering media (power and money) have moved beyond the purview of most critical thinking. Habermas might have missed this because in his account of power he assumes that power is centralized in origin and unidirectional in distribution. Habermas' account of power might benefit from an encounter with the work of Foucault.[331]

## The "New Social Movements"

> In short, the reformed conflicts are not sparked by **problems of distribution**, but concern the **grammar of forms of life**.[332]

Habermas believes that the separation of system and lifeworld, and the rationalization of the lifeworld are ambivalent developments of modern societies. There have been significant gains in freedom. And, social programs are a significant advance in the humaneness of our society. Yet, the mechanisms by which these gains are realized threaten the increases in freedom. The increased intervention of public welfare and legal systems into everyday life has pathological results.

The extension of formal legal systems and public welfare systems into the lifeworld originated in attempts by the state to resolve economic and political crises resulting from increasing inequalities.[333] The state establishes programs aimed at mitigating the social distortion caused by existing class structures.[334] These 'solutions' include programs for public welfare, education, housing, nutrition, legal aid, and so on. These programs have contradictory effects. First, legal and welfare reforms do enhance personal well being and freedom through: allowing and protecting the 'right' to unionize, guaranteeing legal recourse for discrimination, restraining the power of the state apparatus through democratic procedures, and providing economic compensation for those most exploited by economic inequalities.

But, the institutional structures created to enforce claims against the economic and political systems also construct clients and not citizens. As David Ingram notes, an encounter with the legal or welfare bureaucracy " robs the beneficiaries of whatever freedom and dignity they may have gained."[335] The irrationality of legal and welfare reforms (and in existing economic and political systems) consists in the contradiction(s) between the enabling goals and their oppressive implementation. The legislation and programs designed to enhance freedom are implemented in ways which organize/construct the beneficiaries as dependents and clients and not as participants and citizens.[336]

In this way such 'reforms' require that symbolic reproduction functions be subordinated to system integration mechanisms, economic and administrative imperatives increasingly have priority over the values and goals of the lifeworld. These interventions and disruptions of the communicatively organized symbolic reproduction of everyday life threaten personal and collective identities and social crises develop.[337]

When Lukacs described the ways in which the alienation characteristic of life under capitalism moved out of the factories and invaded our everyday life, he identified the process of reification, and unknown to him at the time provided an expansion of Marx's account of alienated labor. We have seen various attempts by members of the Frankfurt School to update Lukacs' account to better fit changing material conditions. Habermas is attempting yet another rewriting of Marx's account of alienation. For Habermas the problem is less one of social relations becoming thingified than one of social relations, especially communicative relations, being organized in ways that impinge on the autonomy of individual and collective identity. He is interested in the "system-induced pathologies of the life-world,"[338] brought about by the one-sided development of modern societies (and the one-sided rationalization of modernity) through a process he calls "the colonization of the lifeworld."

In response to this "colonization of the lifeworld," "new social movements" emerge. These movements challenge the crises in symbolic reproduction. For example: they challenge the instrumentalization of education, the commercialization of relationships and life-styles, bureaucratization and legalization of services, and the routinization of politics.[339] Some of these new social movements, such as religious fundamentalism, or Gingrich-style neo-conservativism are reactionary in their demand for an earlier stage of social integration. Some movements, such as the ecology movement, struggle to resist the demands of the system and work toward creating new broadly democratic mechanisms of control over the system (We have, of course, seen much of the radical economic and political import of the environmental movement dissipate in an attempt to convince people that environmentalism requires no changes in daily life and no structural challenges to the system).

According to Habermas the old social movements were primarily class based conflicts and tended to be organized in parties in order to affect change within systems of representational democracy.[340] The new social movements are based primarily in the new middle class and are organized loosely around struggles for human rights, peace, increased democracy, increased possibilities for self-valorization, and quality of life. The new social movements tend to be organized to encourage participatory democracy. In this way, the new social movements attempt to realize in their practice that which they seek in society as a whole.[341]

Habermas notes that unlike earlier forms of social movements, especially the bourgeois and proletarian revolutions, the new social movements make no claims to speak for all of society.[342] These movements that "always remain tied to the particularism of a special form of life," are characterized by the conscious decision to limit their radicalism and motivated by concerns about "well-defined collective identities."[343]

This means that the new social movements are not revolutionary. The progressive movements aim to defend and advance the gains of the rationalized lifeworld, primarily by protecting the space modernity has opened for communicative action. They work to construct autonomous self-organized public spheres.[344] In the words of Stephen White, the aim of the new social movements is to create "enough slack in the system for the ongoing autonomous articulation of plural identities by the groups involved."[345]

When Habermas describes "autonomous public spheres," he means those that are "neither bred nor kept by a political system for purposes of creating legitimation."[346] These public spheres must be independent of the formally organized political system in order to avoid the invasion and normalization (in Foucault's sense) of the organization by the steering medium of power (and, most likely, money as well).

In Chapters V, VI and VII, I outline the beginnings of a critical theory of the work of Jürgen Habermas. In Chapter V, I examine his account of advanced capitalist society and his analysis of the likely crisis points. My intent is to evaluate Habermas' social theory with respect to his goal of constructing a critical social theory with practical intent. In Chapter V, I indicate the blind spots in his present account. In Chapter VI, I evaluate the work of one of the leading social theorists who stand at odds with Habermas, Michel Foucault. I argue that Habermas' theory retains a moment critical for any critical social theory in his attempts to think the totality. Finally, in Chapter VII, I offer some final thoughts on Habermas and on our present situation and the pressing demands for new types of social thought, organization and action.

# CHAPTER V

# TOWARDS A CRITICAL THEORY OF HABERMAS

> I can not imagine any seriously critical social theory without an internal link to something like an emancipatory interest. That is such a big name! But what I mean is an attitude which is formed in the experience of suffering from something man-made, which can be abolished and should be abolished.[347]

At this point, having briefly sketched out Habermas' attempts to theorize the world of late-capitalism, I believe we need to examine Habermas in light of the self-proclaimed goals of his work. That is, I believe we need a Critical Theory of Habermas. My aim in the last three chapters of this essay is to begin that project. My critique will focus on three broad problem areas in Habermas' attempt to reconstruct a critical social theory while, at the same time, indicating those aspects of Habermas' theory that should be retained by any critical social theory. I argue, in Chapter VI, that Habermas retains an important insight from the tradition of Hegel, Marx and Lukacs. I argue that Habermas' efforts to refigure a notion of 'totality' that is effective in analyzing late 20th century multi-national capitalism is a necessary moment in furthering our emancipatory interest. Further, I will indicate some ways in which Habermas' work can benefit from a dialogue with post-structuralist theory. Finally, in Chapter VII, I offer some thoughts on the form of effective political practice in our time, and argue for the necessity of i) coalitions and ii) a clear articulation of progressive alternatives.

Habermas claims his goal is a reconstituted critical social theory with a practical intent. There are many areas in which he falls short, many ways in which his theory does not give the best possible account of our present situation. Such an account is necessary because in order to change our situation it might be helpful to understand our situation.

## The Role of Class Conflict

> Under these conditions [late-capitalism], the designated executor of the socialist revolution, the proletariat as proletariat, has been dissolved.[348]

Habermas follows the lead of Horkheimer and Adorno when he argues that a new historical situation requires a new understanding of the possibilities of social change. Part of Habermas' reconstructed critical theory is his claim that class conflict will no longer happen because the proletariat as revolutionary class has disappeared. Habermas claims that the working class, as such, no longer exists.

When Habermas claims that class conflict will not be a primary force for social change he might be advancing one of three claims:

1) that class conflict no longer exists.
2) that class conflict no longer appears as such.
3) that class conflict, alone, is no longer enough to address the multiplicity of oppressions and colonizations of late-capitalism.

If we read Habermas as making the first claim, that class conflict no longer exists, then we need to discuss "class." Habermas seems to be working with the same strong notion of class found in Lukacs and carried over by the first generation of critical theorists. The strong notion of class includes the claim that the working class is constituted solely by industrial workers. As many theorists have pointed out perhaps "class" should be more loosely defined. Marx himself was aware that the constitution of the working class would change as Capitalism followed its logic of expansion to a global credit 'based' economy.[349]

I suggest that instead of a strict interpretation we understand "class" as something made through the actions and interactions of human beings. The working class is made up of all those who must continue to work for the gain of someone else in order to pay rent, afford health care, eat, and so on. As E.P. Thompson explains in the Preface to *The Making of the English Working Class*:

> [T]he notion of class entails the notion of historical relationship. Like any other relationship, it is a fluency which evades analysis if we attempt to stop it dead at any given moment and anatomize its structure... The relationship must always be embodied in real people and in a real context..... [C]lass happens when some men, as a result of some common experiences (inherited or shared), feel and articulate the identity of their interests as between themselves, and as against other men whose interests are different from (and usually opposed to) theirs.[350]

According to this account, a class does not just exist, it is something constituted by people in their everyday activities, nor does it have an ideal, or 'real', consciousness. Rather, class is a historically and culturally specific relationship made and defined by humans according to common interests.[351] If 'class' is understood in this way, then a claim that the working class no longer exists seems untenable.

Habermas argues that the gains in material wealth brought about by advanced capitalism mean that "exclusion from control over the means of production is no longer . . . experienced subjectively as proletarian."[352]

To continue our discussion of Habermas on 'class conflict', I propose a second reading of his argument that class conflict will no longer happen. Habermas might be arguing that under late-capitalism class conflict still exists, but it doesn't appear as such, if it appears at all. This line of argument fits well with the position Habermas advances in *Legitimation Crisis* and *The Theory of Communicative Action*. One reason class conflict no longer appears as such, at least in some sectors of the '1st World', is that state, economy and society have become so entwined that the source of social pathologies is difficult to locate. Specifically, economic crisis is often understood as a crisis of the state or self.

In claiming that objectively conflicting class interests will not be experienced as such, Habermas is replicating the Hegelian distinction between appearance and reality.[353] If I am unemployed, fail to get a promotion, live in poverty, I am likely to experience this as a personal failure. After all, in the U.S. everyone who works hard can make something of him or herself. Collective and individual problems will not be interpreted as the result of systemic economic problems, but as a personal problem, or as the result of a governmental failure.

James O'Connor has argued that one result of self-blame is a tendency to construct scapegoats.[354] Given this tendency and the objectively increasing concentration of wealth during the past 15 years, it is no surprise that incidents of racist and religious violence have increased, violent crime is at an all time high in this country, religious fundamentalism has experienced a resurgence, and much popular culture is explicitly racist, misogynistic, or homophobic.[355] In this way, energies which might go into overthrowing the present order and constructing new humane human institutions, communities, relationships, is dissipated in conflict with others in our situation. O'Connor's point is that one reason the working class as such does not appear is that the working class is divided against itself.

One reason for this conflict between people who, I argue, have some interests in common, even if only the interest in doing away with a shared source of oppression, is that in late capitalism the source(s) of oppression is (are) increasingly difficult to identify. This point is one of the themes which runs from Marx through Lukacs, Horkheimer, Adorno and Marcuse to Habermas. Our inability to identify the sources, or contributing factors, of pathological social and individual lives is no accident; it is built into the very structure of capitalism and inserted into our lives through the commodity form.

Finally, it still seems true, in spite of the recently heralded 'death of communism', that for many people in many parts of the world the best entry into progressive politics is through class politics. Consider, for example, this story told by Gabriel Ixmata about the experiences of Guatamalan workers:

> [O]n the coffee plantations, the foremen, stewards, and administrators have their controls, mistreating us, and saying that we must accept what the owner says - and we do - because it is thanks to the owner that there is work for so many people . . .. In the areas where the guerrilla organizations are strong and can exert pressure, the rich are forced to pay higher wages and provide better treatment to the workers. But in those areas where pressure is not exerted by the guerrilla organizations, the o wners p ay m iserable w ages, t reat u s c ruelly, a nd c onstantly c all the army to control and persecute the workers.[356]

This certainly seems to be a case of class conflict that is understood as class conflict by those involved. Although even this apparently clear statement of class antagonism contains the claim that workers should be grateful for the gift of work.[357]

Perhaps this misses the point. Or, at least, perhaps this misses Habermas' point. Perhaps he is only concerned with providing an account of late-capitalism in the '1st world'. If this is the case, then the exportation of much production to the periphery of the '1st world' means that in our struggles we need not focus attention on class conflict because it is relatively insignificant for our situation. Leaving aside for now the manner in which this position only defers the problem to another place and a later time, even near the center of late capitalism (geographically) we find class based organizing playing an important part in progressive politics.

Staughton Lynd has outlined the manner in which a progressive movement has been built in Youngstown, Ohio. This movement began in a democratically organized 'Workers' Solidarity Club'.[358] Lynd describes the result:

> In a community with no organized left presence, a growing number of workers have come to identify with the left's most fundamental perspectives: anti- imperialism, acted out by workers who use their vacations to do skilled labor in Nicaragua; anti- racism and feminism; and most important, a thorough going anti-capitalism, together with unblinking openness to what amount to socialist alternatives.[359]

If we read Habermas as claiming that class conflict no longer appears as such we must ask, "To whom does class conflict not appear as class conflict?" The above recounted stories suggest that some people involved in challenges to existing class structures do understand the economic/class component of the struggle.

In *The Hidden Injuries of Class*, Richard Sennett and Jonathan Cobb survey the discourse about workers' struggles. They note that nonworkers involved "in the argument about workers, rebellion, and culture think more simplistically about workers than workers think about themselves."[360] What Sennett and Cobb find is that all parties in the discussion, including workers who have given up and become conservative and excluding those still involved in working class struggles, fail to acknowledge workers' self-descriptions.[361]

If we read Habermas as claiming that class conflict will not appear as such, then he may be guilty of articulating a theoretical position that is compatible the perspective of those in power. Not necessarily a crime unless one claims to be contributing to the continuing process of human liberation and articulates a theoretical account which denies a still important avenue for such struggle.[362]

On the third proposed reading, Habermas might be claiming that although class struggle still exists and still contains the potential to radically transform the capitalist mode of production, a class based struggle (as traditionally conceived within the Marxist tradition) will not necessarily address all of our problems, nor will it capture the consciousness of enough people to bring about radical change. Recall that the new social movements arise in response to a wide variety of colonizations of a communicatively structured lifeworld. While many of these concerns might be traced to economic factors, it isn't clear that all struggles against the system are economically motivated. The line which Habermas is pushing might be that in order to achieve the sorts of social change envisioned by his theory, in order to affect an emancipation for all people, our movement must be attentive to a whole range of "non-economic" issues (racism, sexism, ableism, ageism, homophobia, etc).

Evidence for this point can be found if we again turn our attention to the recent history of Poland. Here we can find evidence that it is possible for a certain sort of class based movement to be inattentive to the concerns of many of its members (in this case women) and thus fail to achieve the goal of a free society. Since the late 1980s there have been repeated attempts to outlaw all abortions. Combine that with the steadily decreasing role for women in the national government, decreased funding for day care facilities and Church pressure against contraception, and we can easily understand why many Polish women do not perceive the ouster of the Communist Party bureaucracy as the end of their struggles. In fact, many women claim that their situation is being made worse under the rule of a government swept into power under the banner of 'liberation.' We must ask, " Liberation for whom?"

I believe that Habermas' position is something like this last. He understands that privileging class is no guarantee of a free society. Habermas also seems correct, at least partially under readings numbers 1 and 2. That noted, I believe we should read Habermas' account of the colonization of the lifeworld and his theory of communicative action as building on and expanding the accounts of critical left political economy. His lack of attention to class conflict is an attempt i) to be descriptively correct (and in this he is only partially successful), and ii) attentive to the movements of history and the new demands of those engaged in struggles for emancipation.

Habermas' account of the ideal communicative community is supposed to play the role of a normative ideal in his theory.[363] Furthermore, as a regulative normative ideal for social organization, the ideal communicative community should allow for all competing interests to be heard and avoid the sorts of exclusions now taking place in Poland. Unfortunately, Habermas' theory fails on precisely these grounds. In the next section I discuss how it is that Habermas' account of the ideal communicative community turns out to be exclusionary.

## Making Concrete "The Lifeworld"

Habermas' second 'failure' is one of descriptive accuracy. That is, Habermas' lack of a 'deep' or 'thick' account of the lifeworld is neither the most accurate nor helpful account for understanding (and, perhaps informing) the new social movements. By that I mean that his account is not material enough. His appeal to certain abstract conditions for idealized communication doesn't take into account how these conditions might be constructed by actually existing social agents. For this reason his account is only partial (but not false) in a descriptive sense. Furthermore, if attention to the concrete material aspects of the lifeworld is necessary to understanding the ways in which systemic colonization distorts everyday life, then this account must also be considered partial in a political sense. After all, having a "map" of the colonization is helpful in organizing the most effective resistance.

When I claim that Habermas has failed to provide a 'thick' account of the lifeworld I am referring to the sorts of accounts that result from following what Nancy Fraser calls "in-order-to relations."[364] As she explains, when we enter into a political discussion much of what we are contesting is needs interpretation. That is, we are debating what counts as a need, what counts as satisfying a need, who gets to decide. Fraser discusses homelessness and the need for shelter as an example of following out in-order-to relations. When we consider a general need such as the need for shelter, most people will agree that this is a human need and that it ought to be satisfied. But, what counts as shelter? A heating grate near the White House, a bunk at the local shelter, a permanent home? If we decide that homeless people deserve a permanent home, what kind of home is appropriate? How will they pay the rent? Perhaps we should provide job training. But, many homeless adults have children and will need affordable, safe and convenient child care. In order to get to work people may need access to public transportation. Even if we can answer all of these questions, we must then decide how to provide these goods. As Fraser points out, following out these relations entails "proliferating controversy." Following out these chains may mean challenging basic assumptions of our society.

A quick perusal of *The Theory of Communicative Action* will reveal that Habermas does not provide this sort of account. But, he isn't intending to. Perhaps Habermas has provided us a theoretical account that allows space for 'thick' accounts of needs interpretation. This is, I think, one of his goals in positing an ideal speech situation. One of the aims of Habermas' work is to articulate a theoretical account of the possibilities for social change that is attentive to the multiplicity of demands and interests within contemporary society. Old fashioned deterministic class based models of social change are outmoded, in part, because they are exclusionary, such a revolution would not realize the emancipatory goals of all people. I have indicated in my discussion of environmental movements one way in which participants in new social movements might construct 'thick' accounts in practice.[365] This process is an example of the sorts of movements (and the emancipatory potential of movements) that Habermas identifies.

Nonetheless, I believe that Habermas' account of the lifeworld and of social change in late-capitalism is exclusionary, because, in part, it is too general. Seyla Benhabib argues that universalistic moral theories that are based on an abstract ideal of disembodied moral autonomy are exclusionary.[366] Theories of this sort, from Kohlberg's to Rawls' or Locke's, require a certain conception of self and other in which specificity of needs, desires, and historical/cultural location is morally irrelevant. This conception Benhabib, following Mead, calls "the standpoint of the generalized other."[367] From this standpoint we are concerned with what we, as rational beings, have in common. She explains:

> Our relation to the other is governed by the norms of **formal equality** and **reciprocity**: each is entitled to expect and assume from us what we can expect and assume from him or her. The norms of our interactions are primarily public and institutional ones. . . . In treating you in accordance with these norms, I confirm in your person the rights of humanity and I have a legitimate claim to expect that you will do the same in relation to me.[368]

This description might have been written by Habermas to describe the persons constructed by the rationalization of both system and lifeworld. According to Habermas, when the process of constructing such people is distorted (i.e.: when the reproduction of the lifeworld is colonized), then political struggle ensues. On this account, the struggle is over the rights of people **as human**.

To the standpoint of the generalized other Benhabib contrasts:

> The standpoint of the concrete other .... In assuming this standpoint, we abstract from what constitutes our commonality. We seek to comprehend the needs of the other, his or her motivations, what s/he searches for, and what s/he desires. Our relation to the other is governed by norms of **equity** and **complementary reciprocity**: each is entitled to expect and to assume from the other forms of behavior through which the other feels recognized and confirmed as a concrete individual being with specific needs talents and capacities.... The norms of our interaction are usually private, noninstitutional ones.... These norms require in various ways that I exhibit more than the simple assertion of my rights and duties in the face of your needs. In treating you in accordance with the norms of friendship, love and care, I confirm not only your humanity but your human **individuality**.[369]

Under universalist moral and political theories the standpoint of the concrete other is supposed to be irrelevant, or, even worse, irrational. The standpoint of the generalized other is appropriate in public life, and the standpoint of the generalized other is appropriate in the nonpolitical private realm.

Translating this discussion into Habermas' theory we find that people react to social pathologies by organizing movements to affect change on the social system. Habermas replicates the distinction between general and concrete other when he draws on Kohlberg's theory of moral development in order to identify one of the positive affects of rationalization on individuals. One of the advantages of modernity is the construction of (relatively) autonomous individuals who (ideally) interact as equals in the public sphere.

One of the consequences of Habermas' account of the system and lifeworld is that the 'political' and the 'official economy' are contrasted with the 'private', the 'domestic' and the 'home economy'. Nancy Fraser argues that this move serves to exclude domestic concerns from the realm of the political or the economic and thus from the terrain for struggle.[370] Privileging the standpoint of the 'generalized other' is exclusionary and it removes needs interpretation from the sphere of contested discourse. As Iris Young notes, if we examine the history of democracies all too often we find that "the idea of citizenship is the same for all translated in practice to the requirement that all citizens be the same."[371] From the standpoint of the generalized other, needs are irrelevant. This can only mean that what counts as a need and how to satisfy it is noncontroversial. As I have argued, this is not the case. If we accept the standpoint of the generalized other as the only appropriate location from which to evaluate or social order, then the history of ourselves, as well as the pathological character of present gender relations remains beyond questioning.

Habermas does identify the feminist movement as perhaps the new social movement that embodies the liberatory potential of the enlightenment.[372] As Nancy Fraser points out, the system/lifeworld distinction and Habermas' unidirectional account of power are not up to the task of analyzing women's oppression.[373] Susan Hekman argues that Habermas "seem[s] eager to "liberate" women," but only "by turning women into the modernist version of men: rational autonomous and objective."[374]

What I am suggesting, is that Habermas needs to be attentive to the ways in which the lifeworld itself can be a terrain for struggle and liberation. I am also making a stronger claim. This critique has implications for the manner in which we organize our movement (and our everyday lives) as well as implications for what counts as appropriately political. Carole Pateman, Jane Mansbridge and Amy Gutmann all discuss how participatory democratic institutions tend to exclude the voices of women, blacks, and working class people.[375] This happens when the institutions guarantee that everyone will be heard, but only if everyone speaks in the correct manner, follows the rules, and agrees to be rational. In this way even organizations which appear to be radically unlike most existing organizations, and which appear in their very structure to pose a challenge to systemic colonization legitimated by an army of experts, even these participatory organizations replicate the oppression present in the larger society.

Another manner in which Habermas' account of the colonization of the lifeworld fails to be as concrete as it can be, and thereby replicates some already existing social exclusions, stems from his account of power and money as steering media. Money is the form of economic capital and power is the form of political capital in late-capitalism. Leaving aside for the moment the problems with his account of power, this account still seems incomplete. In the political realm we play the roles of citizen, participant, representative, and so on. When these public roles are distorted (for example, citizens become clients) by the attempts of the political system to resolve legitimation crises, then resistance movements are born. What Habermas does not clearly acknowledge, and this is related to his privileging the standpoint of the generalized other, is the deformations, oppression, effects of the differential distribution of what Pierre Bourdieu calls "cultural capital."[376]

One important aspect of bourgeois self-legitimation is the notion of 'merit'. Bourdieu explains:

> Being unable to invoke the right of birth (which their class through the ages has refused the aristocracy) or Nature which, according to "democratic" ideology represents universality, that is to say the ground on which all distinctions are abolished, . . . they can resort to cultivated nature and culture become nature.[377]

Aspects of bourgeois culture that a person learns how to appropriate are presented as available to all (perhaps in museums) and as having value, meaning, or a mystical power to address the 'human spirit' independent of any particular historical or cultural location. The very 'objective' standards by which we evaluate merit, ability to perform (or fit in), and value, are themselves cultural products. And, not surprisingly given the differential distribution of other forms of capital, some of us are given the means to closely approximate these norms, to appropriate various cultural forms to our advantage. In this way, the continual resacralization of culture and art serves to legitimate the existing social order.[378]

Bourdieu describes this process:

> To enable educated men to believe in barbarism and persuade their barbarians within the gates of their own barbarity, all they must do is to manage to conceal themselves and to conceal the social conditions which render possible not only culture as second nature in which society recognizes human excellence or "good form" as the "realization" in a **habitus** of the aesthetics of the ruling classes, but also the legitimized predominance (or, if you like, legitimacy) of a particular definition of culture.[379]

The function of cultural capital is to separate, by an invisible and thereby 'natural' barrier, those who have from those who have not. Evidence of this is found in studies of who goes to museums, concerts, art galleries, and in the attitudes people express about such places.

Working class visitors to the temples of bourgeois culture tend to be significantly few in number in spite of the 'public' character of many such spaces, and they often explicitly express their feelings of discomfort and exclusion. In and of itself this is not necessarily problematic. However, when coupled with the valorization of a certain type of art and merit attached to appreciating such art, these exclusions serve the function of legitimating social inequalities.

As Bourdieu argues in *Distinctions*, cultural capital ranges far beyond the museums and concert halls. The role of making evaluative distinctions carries over into the design of living spaces, the types of food eaten, where the food is purchased, what games are played,[380] what sorts of beverages are consumed, what is worn or driven, how one speaks, who one sleeps with. These distinctions are related to economic situation, and political power. But, as Bourdieu explains, cultural distinctions are not identical to political and economic distinctions. Each of these cultural distinctions serves to legitimate the way of life of those in power and those with money and to exclude others unless they are willing, and lucky enough, to learn the game. The answers a person gives to these sorts of questions mark him or her as hip or square, redneck or cultured, stupid or smart, hippy or solid citizen, bohemian or conformist, educated or ignorant, homosexual or bisexual or 'normal', one of 'us' or one of 'them'. It isn't at all clear how formal struggles for political or economic equality will resolve these forms of making oppressive distinctions.[381]

Again, the problem lies not in the differences as such, but in the fact that we live in a culture which claims to value difference while perpetuating hierarchies of needs, values, interpretations, lifestyles, and so on. In spite of his mention of oppositional cultural movements,[382] it isn't clear that Habermas' account helps us understand the deformations caused by the differential distribution of cultural capital that is entwined with, but not identical to the differential distribution of power and money. To explain this point, we must once again return to the system/lifeworld distinction.

## The "Ideology of the New Class"[383]

Finally, Habermas at times seems to be a sociologist, at times an academic philosopher, and at other times to be a theoretically inclined political activist. That is, it is not always clear when he believes himself to be describing existing conditions and when he thinks he is providing a map for social change. This problem often does make him sound like an apologist for "the ideology of the new class." As such, his entire work serves as "a strategy of containment," one that limits our ability to grasp the possibilities for radical change which do exist, and one which might (in the same way McLuhan's supposedly revolutionary theory did) aid and abet capital in its maintenance of control.

In *The Future of Intellectuals and the Rise of the New Class*, Alvin Gouldner explains the notion of a 'new class' as identifying those who can exploit and benefit from their ability to provide labor to the markets of the "Culture of Critical Discourse."[384] These people are the experts identified by Habermas as one of the results of the process of rationalization. Gouldner argues that the new class has two parts: technical intellectuals and cultural intellectuals. Through a growing emphasis on credentials, appropriate education and professionalization, the new intellectuals assist capitalist domination by furthering the commodification of knowledge and education.

Cornelis Disco argues that Habermas' account of the dialectic of history follows the traditional Marxist dialectic between modes of production and relations of production. Disco explains:

> 1) the forces of production evolve with the accretion of technical knowledge (domination of nature) and organizational knowledge (domination of humans); 2) the relations of production evolve independently with the accretion of moral-practical knowledge in the direction of "greater democracy," based on self-actualization.[385]

This description roughly parallels Habermas' account of the system/lifeworld distinction. Disco argues that the ability to enter into rational discussions about the relations of production is the privilege of the cultural intellectual. That is, discussion about the course of the project of human emancipation is the project of the new class. This is so, because only intellectuals have the store of cultural capital necessary to enter into debates in the public sphere. Habermas privileges argumentative discourse as an ideal for the rational discussion of lifeworld goals. I can find no other way to understand his claims that the force of the better argument alone should 'ideally' carry the day. Habermas does argue, in *The Theory of Communicative Action*, that practical discourse should be concrete and collective and emerge within and from existing human communities. Yet, at the same time, practical discourse is portrayed as purely cognitive and intellectual. For this reason Habermas' idealized discourse has been described as "as ideology of power for intellectuals" based on "the new power of discussion."[386]

If the formal constraints on what counts as rational discourse, or appropriate topics for political discussion are exclusionary because they assume a certain amount of acquired cultural capital, then the procedures that Habermas proposes using to arrive at a practical consensus will end up including only some people. Disco suggests these people will turn out to be intellectuals, the new class. To the extent that this is correct, then Habermas' theory is indeed an ideological justification for the new class, and his account of the new social movements is an account of what Rick Roderick has called "Yuppie Reform Movements"[387] which will not, ultimately affect any systemic change.

Dieter Misgeld has accused Habermas of ignoring the critical knowledge that is always available within the lifeworld. This argument is similar to my argument that Habermas is relatively inattentive to the existence of working class resistance and organization. Misgeld goes further to argue that the system/lifeworld distinction "detracts from the practical point of the theory and blocks reflection upon actual social situations."[388] Misgeld claims that we can never escape the lifeworld and that Habermas' attempt to provide a theory of the colonization of the lifeworld neglects the continual ongoing process of emancipation within the lifeworld.

While I do agree that Habermas tends to ignore struggles within the lifeworld, as well as the possibility for a social crisis originating in lifeworld conflicts, Misgeld's claim that lifeworld based social analyses are critical seems to be naught but a version of Gadamer's hermeneutics and thereby subject to Habermas' critique of hermeneutics.

Nonetheless, Misgeld is addressing the same concern as Disco. Both wonder why it is necessary to have an expert present an account of society before us in order to understand our situation and engage in emancipatory struggles.[389]

This reading of Habermas' theory of the process of forming critical consciousness is similar to what Paulo Friere calls the "banking model" of education. This is the traditional model of education where knowledge is poured into students from the expert teacher. In this context knowledge is "a gift bestowed by those who consider themselves knowledgeable upon those whom they consider to know nothing."[390] This model of education, including educating ourselves about the sources of social pathologies, replicates the oppressive society in which we live.

At this point I believe we can understand that Habermas' theory, whatever its faults, does not intend to endorse a banking model. As Habermas argues, "in a process of enlightenment there can be only participants."[391] Habermas model of discursive struggle and organization allows space for many lifeworld concerns to be voiced. This model is close to Friere's model for a pedagogy of the oppressed: "a pedagogy which must be forged with, not for, the oppressed in the incessant struggle to gain their humanity."[392] Such a process of organizing and educating focuses on revealing the forces at work in everyday life that are either unacknowledged or denied by official accounts of social reality.

Given Habermas' discursive model of organizing and educating, why does he also privilege a form of discourse that excludes many of those his theory professes to assist?

One reason for this apparent blind spot in Habermas' theory is the emphasis he places on systems theory. In "Complexity or Democracy, or the Seducements of Systems Theory," Thomas McCarthy comments:

> Habermas once criticized Marx for succumbing to the illusion of rigorous science, and he traced a number of Marx's historical problems with political analysis and political practice to this source. The question I have wanted to pose here is whether in flirting with systems theory he does not run the danger of being seduced by the same illusion in more modern dress.[393]

The primary problem here is that Habermas just grants the entirety of the social system to the sort of instrumental rationality analyzed by Horkheimer and Adorno in *Dialectic of Enlightenment*. Then, Habermas attempts to use a product of that sphere, systems theory, to understand the role played by the social system in contemporary society. I think Habermas' claim is that our situation is so complex that we need scientific instrumental management techniques in order to keep things running. Furthermore he claims that we need scientific instrumental theories to understand existing political and economic realities.

That *may* be correct. But, this account does ignore the fact that determining what gets to count as the objects of theory and science is a terrain for struggle. McCarthy describes the dangers of Habermas' fascination with systems theory by pointing out that Habermas' analysis of system and lifeworld eliminates the utopian content that must be a part of any emancipatory social theory. The aims and goals of systemic techniques cannot be self-generating or we end up with an Ellul-like pessimism and technological determinism about our taking conscious control of history.[394]

On Habermas' account we struggle to maintain our control over the lifeworld, but only in circumstances when the 'normal' reproduction of everyday life is no longer possible. But, we must then ask, "can we direct/set the goals of the system by other that instrumental means?"

Habermas wants to argue that life-world imperatives ought to give direction to the system.

> Personally, I no longer believe that a differentiated economic system can be transformed from within in accordance with the simple recipes of workers' self-management. The problem seems to be rather one of how capacities for self-organization can be sufficiently developed in autonomous public spheres for the goal-oriented decision-making processes of a use-value oriented life-world to hold the systemic imperatives of economic system and state apparatus in check, and to bring **both** media- controlled subsystems into dependence on life-world imperatives.[395]

One problem here is the notion of "autonomous public spheres." Nancy Fraser has described the ways in which Habermas' account of the bourgeois public sphere[396] describes a situation in which "private people" discuss "public matters."[397] Fraser argues that in order to critique existing democracies, and to anticipate a more fully realized democracy, we must reconstruct the notion of a public sphere to include "interests and issues that bourgeois masculinist ideology labels "private" and treats as inadmissible."[398] Public spheres are always located in time and place, constituted according to the interests of different publics, and will, in any nonhomogeneous society, be multiple. Habermas' account of the public sphere as a privileged sphere for discourse, replicates the exclusion we have been examining throughout this chapter.

Another problem which emerges from Habermas' fetishization of systemic rationality is that Habermas seems inclined to argue that the most likely sites for struggle, the most likely sites for capitalism to generate a crisis lie between system and lifeworld. But, what if the social system generates crisis internally? In recent works William Greider, Claus Offe and James O'Connor demonstrate ways in which the system, specifically the economy, is in fact still generating contradictions and crisis.[399]

What if the lifeworld creates crisis? As discussed above, many demands on the system arise not from a reaction to colonization but from the experiences of people struggling against oppression within the lifeworld. In the next chapter we will examine Foucault's account of power. To the extent that Foucault is descriptively correct, the continual circulation of power through micropractices might mean that the lifeworld itself can be the site of and source of crises and struggle.

Finally, again referring to Foucault, Habermas' use of the system/lifeworld distinction to account for social pathologies requires that we be able to distinguish a normal lifeworld from a pathological lifeworld. Perhaps we can distinguish a normal and pathological lifeworld. Habermas attempts to do so by demonstrating the manner in which money and power function to subordinate the lifeworld to systemic logic. However, if Foucault is correct and the lifeworld cannot be separated from power relations, then how do we determine which, if any, possible lifeworld is 'normal'?

This decision cannot be arbitrary, nor can it be based on so-called objective criteria that turn out to serve the interests of some people and not others. We must choose from those possibilities open to us from our present situation.[400] In the next chapter I will examine some alternative accounts of our present situation and the present possibilities for radical social change.

# CHAPTER VI

## THINKING THE TOTALITY: HABERMAS AND POST-STRUCTURALISM

In this Chapter I argue that at a certain level of abstraction Habermas provides a theory that is more useful than post-structuralist theory -- the primary "big name" rival for attention on the left -- in thinking about political and social change. My example of post-structuralist theory in this essay will be the work of Foucault. One reason I argue that Habermas' account is more useful is his continued attempts to "think the totality." I will make this claim inspite of Habermas' own claims to be avoiding totalizing thought. Like Adorno, Habermas provides us an account of social totality in spite of a suspicion of totalizing thought, and a recognition of the danger of sliding into totalitarianism.[401]

Habermas is concerned that a theory with totalizing claims cannot be made to fit with empirical research.

> The engagement with analytic philosophy, and also the positivist dispute, then reinforced my doubts about whether concepts of totality, of truth, and of theory derived from Hegel did not represent too heavy a mortgage for a theory of society which should also satisfy empirical claims.[402]

One reason that Habermas expresses this suspicion of theorizing totalities is that "[t]otalities only appear in the plural, and this pluralism cannot be anticipated in theory."[403]

One virtue of post-structuralist theory is its attention to diversity. Post-structuralist theory is attentive to plurality that it attempts to instantiate in a theory without a macrotheory (i.e.: a theory which has no theory of totality). In one sense post-structuralist theory is an attempt to anticipate in theory the plurality of totalities to which Habermas refers. The politics that they articulate, a politics which is attentive to and arises from this plurality is a 'micropolitics.' In spite of these intentions post-structuralist theory itself engages in macrotheory. Two of the wellsprings of post-structuralism, Nietzsche and Heidegger, both have macrotheories: Heidegger's about Being, and Nietzsche's about the types of humans and the fate of the humanity.

The refusal to engage in macrotheory (or theorizing the totality) is to buy (quite literally) one of the myths of postmodernity and thus, of late-capitalism. The myth of postmodernity is that history (or politics, or ideology...) is at an end. As I discuss in the next section, such an explicit refusal to engage in political or historical discourse often obscures a macrotheory with conservative, if not reactionary, political implications.

## Refiguring "Power": Michel Foucault

> If you ask me, "Does this new technology of power take its historical origin from an identifiable individual or group of individuals who decide to implement it so as to further their own interests or facilitate their utilization of the social body?" then I would say "No". These tactics were invented and organized from the starting points of local conditions and particular needs.[404]

Foucault has been accused of having no positive politics. I argue that when there is a positive politics that follows from post-structuralist theory the 'micropolitical' struggles might affect reform, but systemic changes will be beyond their reach. To explain this point I will focus on Foucault's account of power and the political implications of his theory.[405]

Foucault, like Habermas, claims that power, modern power as a medium of control and domination had its origins in local, lifeworld concerns. In the late 18th century a variety of "microtechniques" were developed in schools, hospitals and prisons far from the traditional centers of power. Only later would these techniques be utilized in global strategies of domination.[406]

Foucault characterizes modern power as "disciplinary power" in part because of its origins in disciplinary institutions which first faced the problems of organizing, managing, watching and controlling large numbers of persons. Later these problems would become central problems for modern governments and they would take up the practices developed at the fringes of the old society. Previously power had its location in the person of the sovereign. By contrast, modern power "has its principle not so much in a person as in a certain concerted distribution of bodies, surfaces, lights, gazes; in an arrangement whose internal mechanisms produce the relation in which the individuals are caught up."[407]

One of the disciplinary practices that Foucault discusses is "the gaze." The gaze allows administrators to manage their institutions by organizing the populations so that they could be watched, known, and controlled. This watching took place on two levels and required constructing two new objects of knowledge --the social group and the individual.

In *The Birth of the Clinic*, Foucault recounts the origin of the "medical gaze." This gaze was made possible by the intersection of i) the construction of the individual as a "case" and the new types of detailed observation made possible by the bedside observation in modern hospitals; with ii) the arrangements and segregation of patients in accord with the types of diseases (witness many proposals for dealing with PWAIDS) and systems of monitoring health at the state level which though semi-autonomous (AMA) are centralized authorities "for the recording and assessment of all medical activity."[408]

Twelve years later when *Discipline and Punish* appeared we find Foucault once again taking up "the gaze." In this text his central example of the creation of a modern "economy of power" is Bentham's Panopticon. The Panopticon is a model for prison design consisting of rings of backlit cells surrounding a central elevated watchtower. This design allows a single guard to oversee many inmates and provides a single objective view of the members of prison society and their relations. Because the cells are backlit, the inmates can tell neither when they are being observed, how many observers there are, nor even if they are ever being watched. The effect is to create self-policing prisoners. Foucault observes,

> The efficiency of power, its constraining force have, in a sense, passed over to the other side -- to the side of its surface of application. He

> who is subjected to a field of visibility, and who knows it, assumes responsibility for the constraints of power; he makes them play spontaneously upon himself; he inscribes in himself the power relation in which he simultaneously plays both roles; he becomes the principle of his own subjection.[409]

What happens is that the prisoners internalize the gaze and police their own behavior. Throughout modern institutions, in hospitals, prisons, schools, this type of observation objectifies its targets and invades their lives. The rationalization process described by Weber and Habermas is, on Foucault's understanding, a new mode of social control.

With the rise of modern societies comes the "necessity to ensure the circulation of effects of power through progressively finer channels, gaining access to individuals themselves, to their bodies, their gestures and all their daily actions."[410] Disciplinary power is always already everywhere; it is in us, in our desires, our habits, our bodies. Modern power is, in Foucault's words, capillary. Furthermore, it is "self-amplifying," it aims not at suppression but at the reconstruction of its objects.

## Some Political Implications of Foucault's Account

> There aren't immediately given subjects of the struggle... Who fights against whom? We all fight each other. And there is always within each of us something that fights something else.[411]

If Foucault is correct, if power is capillary in character, then power is as present in aspects of daily life (cooking, choosing which clothes to wear, dating) as it is in system of bureaucratic/administrative organization.

If Foucault is correct, then power is decentered and continuous. In fact, power is itself not a unitary notion, power is multiple and encompasses such diverse phenomena as criteria for knowledge claims and the secret and coercive extraction of knowledge from and about persons.

"Power is everywhere" argues Foucault.[412] One claim that follows from this is that we are always already engaged in struggles for the structure and meaning of our daily life. The politics that follows from this claim is a politics structured around single issues and local demands (abortion rights, or neighborhood politics). These struggles are "micro-politics."

## Thinking the Totality: Habermas and Post-Structuralism   113

One of the problems with Foucault's account of power and resistance is the claim that we are always already involved in power relations that cannot, in the final instance, be transformed. Thus, we are left with a politics characterized by Nancy Fraser as a politics "of multiple local resistances carried out in the name of no articulable positive ideal."[413] Such a politics doesn't, in spite of Foucault's claims to the contrary,[414] offer much hope for systemic change.

Foucault may not be claiming that some set of actually existing power relations is inescapable. Rather, Foucault might be arguing that it is impossible to escape all power relations. That is, that some relations of power will exist. Power relations are, after all, constitutive of human being on this account. If this is a plausible reading, then the role played by power in Foucault and the role of linguistic relations in Habermas are roughly analogous -- at least with respect to the constitution of subjectivity. The goal of struggle for social change will be to identify those relations which have a distorting effect on human being and which should be changed.

This takes us, I believe, to a crucial difference between Habermas' account of power and Foucault's. For Foucault power is non-normative and everywhere. So, how is it possible to resist, or to know what to resist. But, as Habermas notes, the questions raised by Foucault's account go even deeper:

> If it is just a matter of mobilizing counterpower, of strategic battles and wily confrontations, why should we muster any resistance at all against this all-pervasive power circulating in the bloodstream of the body of modern society, instead of just adopting ourselves to it?... why fight at all?[415]

If the colonization of the lifeworld is a systematic, though 'subjectless', matter, and none of the theorists discussed have given us any reason to believe otherwise, then systemic changes are necessary. Habermas does talk about the possibility of change at the level of the social whole. That is, Habermas continues to think the totality. This is necessary because,

> We cannot but live in a total world. The world constitutes a totality -- inevitably -- in the background of our everyday activities. Now the problem is whether one can employ a theoretical language to analyze a concrete life-world, as a particular totality, or whether one refrains

from that claim and restricts oneself to an analysis of the presumably universal infrastructure which all life-worlds share with each other. It is this infrastructure that I'm interested in.[416]

Systemic changes are necessary if we hope to i) defend the life-world from systemic colonization, or ii) challenge the imperatives which presently structure and drive the system [though Habermas is skeptical about this latter, claiming that at best we might set some goals for the system, but I'm arguing for a more ambitious social theory].  In spite of Habermas' denial of a Hegalianized notion of totality, he wishes to retain a more supple and narratively constituted notion of totality (again, as with the notion of class, we are having to loosen a concept. The fact that Habermas gets this one and misses class lends some credence to the "ideology of the new class" talk, or may be yet again an indication that nobody can do everything.)

Habermas also is successful in identifying one of the ways in which capitalism now generates and solves contradictions and crises -- through thwarting and distorting communicative action  (one interpretation of events in some "easternbloc" countries is that workers didn't want to give up many aspects of socialism, but they did want a voice in public discourse -- a role in defining social goals).[417]

# CHAPTER VII

# SOME CONCLUDING THOUGHTS: SALVAGING CRITICAL THEORY, OR THE NECESSITY OF COALITIONS

> The death of a social machine has never been heralded by a disharmony or a dysfunction. . . . Capitalism has learned this, and has ceased doubting itself, while even socialists have abandoned belief in the possibility of capitalism's natural death by attrition. No one has ever died from contradictions. And the more it breaks down, the more it schizophrenizes, the better it works, the American way.[418]

At this point, after criticizing Habermas' account of colonization for A) ignoring class, B) an insufficiently supple account of the lifeworld, and C) dangerously ceding the level of the social system to systemic rationality; and after valorizing his continued attempt to talk about social wholes, I now offer some suggestions for how we might proceed to salvage that which is useful in Habermas. In salvaging what is useful my goal is neither to praise nor damn Habermas, but to see what, if anything, he tells us which might allow us to reconstruct a critical social theory which might be helpful to progressive politics. I believe we should salvage the "colonization of the lifeworld" thesis (which I will have argued throughout is but a continuation of the attempt to understand i) Marx's account of alienation and ii) the relation between social being and social consciousness).

First, when Habermas discusses money and power he has an acceptable account of money and the way it functions in colonizing the lifeworld. Of course, he has the entire tradition of critical political economy to build on. But, his account of power is thin. Habermas' account of the politics of the new social movements is based, in part, on his account of power. For this reason we find that the sites for struggle occur at the interstices of system and lifeworld, that collectivities within the lifeworld resist the invasion of power into the symbolic reproduction of everyday life.

Both Habermas and Foucault agree that just as modern power has its origin in local necessities, so too must resistance. Habermas identifies what he calls "new social movements" (environmentalism, religious fundamentalism, feminism...) and Foucault valorizes "micropolitics." One difference between Habermas' account of the new social movements, and Foucault's account of micropolitical struggles is that on Foucault's version of the emerging politics power does not flow unidirectionally from the system to the lifeworld. This means that Habermas is too quick to locate the system/lifeworld intersection as **the** site for struggle and resistance. Foucault's account means that a liberatory politics will include (begin with?) a politics of everyday life. This is, of course, an argument made by many feminists, radical environmentalists, and other members of "new social movements."

Second, just as Habermas account of power is thin, so too is his notion of the lifeworld. The account of the lifeworld must be concretized if for no other reason than it seems to be a "bad abstraction", one which doesn't pay sufficient attention to the diversity and complexity of everyday life. It can be enriched by drawing on i) Henri Lefebvre and the situationists on everyday life,[419] ii) Dewey and McDermott on the aesthetic of the everyday,[420] iii) Post-structuralist theory (Derrida, Foucault) with its attention to heterogeneity, difference and textuality,[421] and iv) Ingram, Fraser, Roderick, Matustik, Young, Honneth, and others who, working within the Critical Theory tradition, point out the ways in which Habermas' notion of the lifeworld and its colonization continues to privilege an elite Euro-male viewpoint.[422] Habermas is aware of this aspect of his theory. When asked in 1984 by Perry Anderson and Peter Dews if his work had anything to say to socialist liberation struggles in the third world and if critical theory had anything to learn from such struggles, Habermas responded, "I am tempted to say no in both cases. I am aware of the fact that this is a eurocentrically limited view."[423]

I also want to claim that in many spheres of late-capitalism, Habermas' account does work as a critical social theory with respect to some sectors of the '1st world' and with respect to some social movements.[424] In addition, his account of the communicative demands for a public sphere seems accurate (at least partially) in parts of Eastern Europe and China.

Finally, I want to suggest that in order to read Habermas as a revolutionary, as one committed to radical social change (and not as yet another sophisticated 'objective' information theorist or sociologist) is to contextualize his work, to read it, as I have, within an ongoing tradition. In spite of the breadth and complexity of his concerns, we need to read his work as an opening up of theories of the relation between being and consciousness, and as a reworking of the Marxist tradition of attempts to rethink the base/superstructure relation.[425] Here we should note the workers' resistance to privatization in Eastern Europe. There are demands for something like a 'public sphere', just as a Habermasian might expect. In addition, there also exists resistance (much of it local) to privatization of the means of production and distribution.

## The Necessity of Coalitions

> Every intervention in complex social structures has such unforeseeable consequences that processes of reform can only be defended as scrupulous process of trial and error under the careful control of those who have to bear their consequences.[426]

The primary problem of a politics in the first days of the 21st century is the problem of coalitions. At some level Habermas' account of new social movements and various poststructuralist accounts of micropolitics are accurate accounts of the actually existing politics, especially in what we might call the core countries of late, or postmodern, capitalism. I think Habermas' account of the "new social movements" can be enriched (rewritten) in the manner described above. Locating a theory of power within an account of a social totality is important because such talk helps parties in different social locations understand what they have in common, why they should build coalitions to accomplish structural systemic change, and in whose name the struggle should take place -- our own.

In "Towards Many Socialisms," Raymond Williams notes that, "[o]n the one hand, the twentieth century has shown us, unmistakably, that we have to think in world-historical ways."[427] At the same time, thinking in this way often obscures the very process we are attempting to understand. "[W]orld history itself," Williams wrote, has shown not only the inappropriateness of the singular and unilinear model but also the underlying truths of the analysis and aspirations which this model had tried to unfold.[428]

This is precisely the dilemma that Habermas faces in his attempt to reconstruct Critical Theory. This is the dilemma all of us face, all of us committed to the project of human freedom must realize that since there are many cultures, needs and interests, that emancipation will take many forms. As Billy Bragg sings, "all revolutions are not the same. They are as different as the cultures which give them birth."[429] Or, to borrow yet again Williams' words, "there will be many socialisms."[430]

In his recent argument for the virtues of a liberal ironist ideal, *Contingency, Irony, and Solidarity*, Richard Rorty claims that what he and Habermas really disagree about is the appropriate "self-image" of a democratic society. As Rorty notes, Habermas believes a democratic society must aim at universalism.[431] It seems to me that Habermas' emphasis on universalism is more than just a self-description of a democratic society.

When he argues for the value of universalism, Habermas is making two sorts of claims. First, he is making a normative claim about the necessity of aspiring to universal norms in order to achieve a free and just society. Second, Habermas is making a claim about the inevitable convergence of rational communication.[432] We have already examined the limitations of these claims - the ways in which they can function as bad abstractions, as strategies of containment.

But, Habermas' universalism, his insistence on attempting to think the totality in days like these is useful both politically and heuristically. Habermas' universalism is necessary and useful not because of any claims about shared humanity nor because of any claims about human nature. His theorizing is necessary and useful because, if correct, his account provides us with a tool, a map that traces the common sources of our many different colonizations.

Understanding the common sources of the disparate pathologies we face in our lifeworld today may help motivate/explain the necessity of coalitions to affect change. The actual shape of these coalitions, and the shape of the future is not something provided in advance, not something determined by speculating on the decisions of pre- or nonsocial beings, rather it is something worked out through the interactions of situated humans. The continuing struggles do not follow any master blueprint that will lead us to **the** society where humans will realize their true nature. Nor should they, if nothing else this century should have taught us to be wary of master plans which others formulate for our lives, plans which will allow us to recover our 'true' nature. Instead, let us hope that we will move toward a future characterized by Rorty as "an endless, proliferating realization of Freedom[s]."[433]

# NOTES

[1] Karl Marx, "Preface to *A Critique of Political Economy,*" in *Karl Marx: Selected Writings*, ed. David McLellan, [New York: Oxford University Press, 1977], p. 389. As one who accepts the feminist critique of sexist language, I find the language in which most of the figures considered in this essay speak highly problematic. In my own writing I attempt to take account of this critique. In so far as I am successful, thanks are due to Shelley Park and Michelle LaRocque (see Shelley Park and Michelle LaRocque, "What's a Nice Girl Like Me Doing in a Profession Like This," *unpublished manuscript*); in so far as I fail, in this and other matters herein, the shortcomings are of my own construction.

[2] "Western Marxism" is a term used to designate a tradition which begins with Georg Lukacs' *History and Class Consciousness*, [Cambridge, MA: MIT Press, 1971] (hereafter cited as Lukacs, *HCC*), and which rejects both i) the determinism of the Second International and ii) the mid-twentieth Century Stalinist orthodoxy. See Maurice Merleau-Ponty, *Adventures of the Dialectic*, [Evanston: Northwestern University Press, 1973]. See also Perry Anderson, *Considerations on Western Marxism*, [London: Verso, 1979].

[3] In "The Frankfurt School in Exile," *Perspectives in American History* 6, (1972): 340, Martin Jay attributes the first use of the term "critical theory" to Max Horkheimer in his 1937 essay "Traditional and Critical Theory," republished in *Critical Theory: Selected Essays*, trans. Matthew J. O'Connell [New York: Herder and Herder, 1972], pp. 188-243. For a survey of literature through 1980 see Douglas Kellner and Rick Roderick, "Recent Literature on Critical Theory," *New German Critique* 23, (1981): 159-166.

[4] Karl Marx, *Capital*, vol. I: *A Critique of Political Economy*, trans. Ben Fowkes [NY: Vintage, 1977], pp. 164-165.

[5] Marx, *Capital*, Vol. 1, p. 135.

[6] Marx, *Capital*, Vol. 1, p. 135.

[7] The classical political economists did recognize human labor as the source of value and wealth (Locke, Smith, and Ricardo all subscribe to the Labor Theory of Value), but they tend to treat the commodity and its exchange relations as eternal - as if they were discovering economic laws with the same 'natural' and 'objective' basis as the natural sciences. And, as Marx notes, they have, in so far as they offer a correct description of the relations of capitalism.

[8] Here Marx is following Hegel. Hegel argues that appearance is not mere illusion (and thus 'false') but should be understood as the immediate reality of being, as its proximally revealed form (and thus partially 'true'). See, G. W. F. Hegel, *Phenomonology of Spirit*, trans. A. V. Miller [New York: Oxford University Press, 1977], p. 87 (hereafter cited as Hegel, *POS*). See also G. W. F. Hegel, *Logic*, [New York: Oxford University Press, 1982], p. 73, and pp. 186 - 195.

[9] Marx, *Capital*, Vol. I, p. 166.

[10] Marx, *Capital*, Vol. I, p. 167.

[11] Marx, *Capital*, Vol. I, p. 167.

[12] Marx, *Capital*, Vol. I, p. 175.

[13] Marx, *Capital*, Vol. I, p. 131.

[14] For example, Marx describes why it is that the capitalist **should** own the products of labor: "The labour process is a process between things the capitalist has purchased, things which belong to him. Thus the product of this process belongs to him just as much as the wine which is the product of the process of fermentation going on in his cellar." *Capital*, Vol. I, p. 292.

[15] For an extended critique of this tendency in Marx see Jean Baudrillard, *The Mirror of Production*, [St. Louis: Telos Press, 1975] (hereafter cited as Baudrillard, *MOP*). Habermas also claims that Marx overemphasizes production. For a discussion of this critique see Chapters III and IV.

[16] See Paul de Man, *Blindness and Insight: Essays in the Rhetoric of Contemporary Criticism*, [London: Methuen, 1983]. In this book de Man argues that the blind spots in a text often lead us to its deepest insights. It may be that Marx's failure to clearly articulate **the** alternative he envisioned is not only a blind spot and lack in his text, but also reveals an important and desirable limitation on theory. Some postmodern critiques of totalizing thought argue that attempts to think beyond where we are (or, to think too far beyond) do not aid emancipatory projects, but instead are part of such 20th century disasters as Hitler's Reich and Stalin's Soviet Union. I will partially address the problem of "totality" in Chapter VI.

[17] G. W. F. Hegel, *The Philosophy of History*, [New York: Dover Publications, 1956], p. 456.

[18] Hegel, *The Philosophy of History*, especially the "Introduction," pp. 1-109.

[19] See G. W. F. Hegel, *The Philosophy of Right*, [New York: Oxford University Press, 1967].

[20] See Karl Marx, *The German Ideology*, in *Karl Marx: Selected Writings*, [Moscow: Progress Publishers, 1964] (hereafter cited as Marx, *The German Ideology*).

[21] Marx, "Preface to *A Critique of Political Economy*," p. 389.

[22] Marx, *The German Ideology*, p. 57.

[23] Marx describes his differences with Hegel on the content of the dialectic in his 1873 "Postface to the Second Edition" of *Capital:* "With me the reverse is true: the ideal is nothing but the material world reflected in the mind of man, and translated into forms of thought." p. 102.

[24] Karl Marx and Fredrich Engels, *The Communist Manifesto*, in *Karl Marx: Selected Writings*, ed. David McLellan, [New York: Oxford University Press, 1977], p. 222. The account of Marx's theory of history that I have given here is sometimes characterized as the 'continuity account.' For a survey of literature on Marx's account(s) of history and an attempt to reconcile seemingly contradictory aspects see: Steve Best, "Marx and the Problem of Conflicting Models of History," *The Philosophical Forum* 22, (Winter 1990): 167-192. For an explanation of Marx's theory of history and its relation to Hegel within the tradition of analytic philosophy see G. A. Cohen, *Karl Marx's Theory of History: A Defense*, [Oxford: Clarendon Press, 1978].

[25] On "Strategy of Containment" as an issue in theory see Fredric Jameson, *The Political Unconscious* [Ithaca, NY: Cornell University Press].

[26] Karl Popper's theory of science is based on the claim that science works by falsification. In testing theories, examples which confirm the theory do not prove anything, but counterexamples show the theory to be false. This method of evaluating theories, he argues, is applicable to social science. On this ground, he argues that Marxism has been falsified. See his *The Open Society and Its Enemies*, [Princeton, NJ: Princeton University Press, 1966]. This argument may hold against orthodox Marxism, but it does not hold as a critique of critical Marxism since the point of his argument is that history does not unfold according to iron laws but only as made by human agents. As we shall see, this is also the claim of critical theory. In spite of this, Habermas opens "Between Philosophy and Science: Marxism as Critique" with "four facts against Marxism." See Chapter III. A related, but refined account of theory falsification in science can be found in Pierre Duhem. Duhem argues that falsification involves bundles of hypotheses, not a single theoretical structure.

On this account we could argue either i) that some, but not all, of the initial hypotheses of Marxism are false, or ii) that the initial hypotheses of Marxism captured something true about that time and place (and I would argue still true), but stand in need of augmentation in order to account for the limits of the initial theory.

[27] One way to analyze the "crisis of Marxism" is as bound up with the general crisis of Modernity. As we live the last days of the 20th century, can anything motivate us to escape the century of Auschwitz, Biafra, Jonestown, . . . .. See Stanley Aronowitz, *The Crisis in Historical Materialism: Class, Politics and Culture in Marxist Theory*, 2nd ed., forward by Colin MacCabe [Minneapolis: University of Minnesota Press, 1990]; Karl Korsch, in *Karl Korsch: Revolutionary Theory*, ed. Douglas Kellner [Austin: University of Texas Press, 1977]; Alvin Gouldner, *The Two Marxisms*, [New York: Seabury Press, 1980].

[28] Perhaps I should claim, "Or so the story went." With the recent changes in Europe, China, and the former USSR, it seems we have arrived at a new "crisis of Marxism." This situation still demands analysis. For some beginnings in thinking about our new crisis see Stanley Aronowitz, "The Future of Socialism?" *Social Text*, no. 24, (1990), pp. 85-116; Michael Buraway, "Marxism is Dead, Long Live Marxism!" *Socialist Review* 20 (April/June 1990): 7-19; *The Future of Socialism, Monthly Review* 42 (July/August 1990); Toni Negri, "Postscript, 1990," in *Communists Like Us*, by Felix Guattari and Toni Negri, trans. Michael Ryan [New York: Semiotext(e), 1990]. For some neoconservative accounts see "Z", "To the Stalin Mausoleum," *Deadalus* 119, (Winter 1990); Francis Fukuyama, "The End of History?" *The National Interest*, (Summer 1989).

[29] See Louis Althusser, *Reading Capital*, [London: New Left Books, 1970], pp 100ff.

[30] On "Late Capitalism" see Ernst Mandel, *Late Capitalism*, [London: New Left Books, 1975].

[31] Following Henri Lefebvre, I will understand ideology as any practice, including beliefs, which serves to perpetuate existing social structures and to limit possibilities of realizing the possibility of change. See Henri Lefebvre, *Everyday Life in the Modern World*, trans Sacha Rabinovitch [New Brunswick, NJ: Transaction Books, 1984]. See also Louis Althusser, "Ideology and Ideological State Apparatuses," in *Lenin and Philosophy*, [New York: Monthly Review Press, 1971], pp. 127-186.

[32] Vladimir Lenin, "The Three Sources and Component Parts of Marxism," in *Historical Materialism* by Vladimir Lenin, Karl Marx, and Friedrich Engels

[Moscow: Progress Publishers, 1970]. Marx's personal experience with labor organizations played no small role in the formation of his theory.

[33] Immanuel Kant, *Groundwork of the Metaphysic of Morals*, trans. H. J. Paton [New York: Harper Torchbooks, 1956]. See also Immanuel Kant, "What is Enlightenment" in *Kant Selections*, ed. Lewis White Beck [New York: Macmillan, 1988].

[34] Kant, *Groundwork of the Metaphysic of Morals*, pp. 113-120.

[35] For more on the relationship of Kant to this tradition see my discussion of Lukacs' critique of Kant later in this chapter.

[36] Alasdair MacIntyre, *A Short History of Ethics*, [New York: The Macmillan Company, 1971], p. 211.

[37] Hegel, *Logic*, pp. 127-134.

[38] Hegel, *Logic*, p. 127.

[39] Hegel, *Logic*, p. 131.

[40] Marx, *Economic and Philosophic Manuscripts of 1844*, [New York: International Publishers, 1964], pp. 187-188 (hereafter cited as Marx, *EPM*).

[41] Hegel, *POS*, pp. 111-119.

[42] Hegel, *POS*, pp. 111-112.

[43] Albert Camus, "An Absurd Reasoning" in *The Myth of Sisyphus and Other Essays*, [New York: Vintage Books, 1955], p. 3. Hegel was "introduced" to Camus' generation of Frencjh intellectuals by Alexandre Kojev. See Kojev, *Introduction a la lecture de Hegel: lecon sur La phenomenologie de l'espirit, professees de 1933 a 1939 a l'Ecole des hautes-etudes*, [Paris: Gallimard, 1947].

[44] Hegel, *POS*, p. 114.

[45] Hegel, *POS*, p. 114.

[46] See Hegel, *POS*, pp. 104-111.

⁴⁷Robert Solomon, *In the Spirit of Hegel: A Study of G. W. F. Hegel's "Phenomonology of Spirit"*, [New York: Oxford University Press, 1983], p. 452.

⁴⁸Hegel, *POS*, p. 116.

⁴⁹Hegel, *POS*, p. 116.

⁵⁰Hegel, *POS*, p. 119.

⁵¹Hegel, *POS*, p. 488.

⁵²Hegel, *POS*, p. 488.

⁵³See David MacGregor, *The Communist Ideal in Hegel and Marx*, [Buffalo: University of Toronto Press, 1984].

⁵⁴Ludwig Feuerbach, *Principles of the Philosophy of the Future*, [Indianapolis, IN: Hackett, 1986], p. 49.

⁵⁵See Ludwig Feuerbach, *Essence of Christianity*, [New York: Harper and Row, 1957] (hereafter cited as Feuerbach, *EOC*).

⁵⁶See Feuerbach, *Principles of the Philosophy of the Future*.

⁵⁷Karl Marx, "Theses on Feuerbach", in *Marx: Selected Writings*, ed. David McLellan [New York: Oxford University Press, 1987], p. 156 (hereafter cited as Marx, "Theses").

⁵⁸Marx, "Theses," p. 157.

⁵⁹Marx, "Theses," p. 156.

⁶⁰Marx, *EPM*, p. 107.

⁶¹Marx, *EPM*, p. 110.

⁶²Marx, *EPM*, p. 111. This point seems to be missed by both i) many Marxists who so valorize labor they partially justify the criticisms of ii) many critics, such as Jean Baudrillard, who accuse Marx of fetishizing labor. See, Baudrillard, *MOP*.

⁶³Marx, *EPM*, p. 115.

⁶⁴Feuerbach, *EOC*, p. 2.

⁶⁵Feuerbach, *EOC*, pp. 21-29.

⁶⁶Habermas argues, following Kant, that the possibility of thinking in this universalizing fashion is a product of modernity. See Chapters III and IV.

⁶⁷Marx, *EPM*, p. 114.

⁶⁸We might make a distinction between what is economically feasible and what is humanly feasible. For instance, today much food rots and much agricultural production in the 'third world' is devoted to growing luxury items for the U.S. and Western Europe, at the same time many people starve to death or go hungry everyday. We have the capacity to feed every human on this planet, but we can't conceive of this possibility because it isn't "practical." Thus commodity fetishism, economic growth simply for the sake of growth, the privileging of money over life, divides us against each other and limits our ability to grasp common interests and desires, limits the possibility that we will work together to meet these needs (conceivably we could do so in a variety of ways - this argument does not demand a single unitary notion of how we meet our needs, or how we desire that they be met). See Leslie Sklair, *Sociology of the Global System*, [Baltimore: Johns Hopkins University Press, 1991]; "The Business of Hunger," [Videocassette, Maryknoll World Video, 1984].

⁶⁹Karl Marx, *Grundrisse*, [London: Penguin and New Left Review, 1973], p. 611.

⁷⁰Marx, *The German Ideology*, p. 87.

⁷¹Marx, *The German Ideology*, p. 262. As we shall discover, this sort of account will recur throughout the Critical Theory tradition - from Horkheimer and Adorno's identification of the over privileging of instrumentality under capitalism to Habermas' account of the one sided development of the system and its colonization of the lifeworld.

⁷²Evidence of the lingering truth of this claim can be found in many plans for reforming education in the United State in the late 20th century. Increasingly we hear that the way to fix public education is to more deeply involve industrial and corporate "partners" in the educational process. This will include designing curricula aimed at turning out good workers. This may, or may not, be the same as educating creative, whole, critical thinking individual citizens. Another example of the commodification of education is the spate of recent plans to privatize public education that would allow profit making on "public" schools.

[73] For more on subjectless origin of oppression and post-structuralist theory see Chapters IV - VII..

[74] Marx, *The German Ideology*, p. 79. Does Marx mean no actually existing social organization can give workers control of their lives, or that no such organization is even possible? Surely he means the former.

[75] Marx, *The German Ideology*, p. 78. Much has been made recently i) of the lack of community in the United States (and the world -- at a global level), or ii) of the fragile or illusory character of what community there is. For two books which deal with this issue and point toward new ways of thinking and living community see: Bill Martin, *Matrix and Line: Derrida and the Possibilities of Postmodern Social Theory* [Albany: State University of New York Press, 1992]; and Martin Matustik, *Postnational Identity: Critical Theory and Existential Philosophy in Habermas, Kierkegaard and Havel*, [New York: The Guilford Press, 1993].

[76] None of this should be read as implying that Capitalism moves of its own accord. Changes in capitalism tend to be in response to demands and activities of workers and consumers. Capitalism modifies (and extends itself) in an effort to i) answer these demands and ii) thereby maintain its hegemony.

[77] Lukacs, *HCC*, p. 84.

[78] Lukacs, *HCC*, p. xxi. Lukacs finds that in *Capital* "a whole series of categories of central importance and in constant use stem directly from Hegel's *Logic*." *HCC*, p. xliv. In using Hegel to construct a revolutionary reading of Marx, Lukacs was not alone - Lenin claimed that Marxists misunderstood Marx because they knew nothing of Hegel.

[79] Lukacs, *HCC*, p. xxii.

[80] Lukacs, *HCC*, p. 86.

[81] David Held, *Introduction to Critical Theory*, [Berkeley: University of California Press, 1980], p. 65. For more on Weber see Arthur Mitzman, *The Iron Cage: An Historical Interpretation of Max Weber*, [New York: Grosset and Dunlap, 1969].

[82] For Weber's account of the rationalization of religion see: Max Weber, *The Religion of China: Confucianism and Taoism*, [Glencoe, IL: Free Press, 1951]; Max Weber, *Theory of Social and Economic Organization*, [Glencoe, IL: Free Press, 1957]; Max Weber, *The Protestant Ethic and the Spirit of Capitalism*, [New York: Scribner's, 1958] (hereafter cited as Weber, *The Protestant Ethic*).

[83] The rationalization of religion is a necessary but not sufficient condition for the rise of capitalism and secular rationalization. See Max Weber, *General Economic History*, [New York: Greenberg Press, 1927], p. 260; Weber, *The Religion of China*, p. 104.

[84] Max Weber, *From Max Weber: Essays in Sociology*, ed. H. H. Gerth and C. Wright Mills, [New York: Oxford University Press, 1972], p. 139.

[85] Weber, *The Protestant Ethic*, p. 181

[86] Weber, *The Protestant Ethic*, p. 181.

[87] Weber, *Theory of Social and Economic Organization*, p. 224. In making the claim that attempts to change society through revolution will leave many existing problems untouched, Weber is echoing Kant's discussion of revolution and reform in "What is Enlightenment." The notion that attempts at revolution will only further systems of control is clearly rearticulated in the recent work of Baudrillard.

[88] Lukacs, *HCC*, p. 179. The 'mere' appearance of the officially articulated separation of value spheres in culture is often torn apart by everyday activities. For example, the separation of church and state in this country is constantly challenged from both sides - in part because religion, if not the state, of necessity aspires to a give a total account of the world. The current debates about abortion, sex education, and multi-culturalism reveal the arbitrary nature of many cultural categories. This latter is addressed by many feminists who note that formal legal equality has not lead to social equality. See Iris Marion Young, "Polity and Group Difference: A Critique of the Ideal of Universal Citizenship," in *Feminism and Political Theory*, ed. Cass R. Sunstein, [Chicago: University of Chicago Press, 1990], pp. 117 - 141.

[89] "However, all these peculiarities of Western capitalism have derived their significance in the last analysis from their association with the capitalistic organization of labour." Weber, *The Protestant Ethic*, p. 22.

[90] Lukacs, *HCC*, pp. 95-103.

[91] See Harry Braverman, *Labor and Monopolt Capitalism: The Degradation of Work in the Twentieth Century*, [1974].

[92] Lukacs, *HCC*, p. 89.

[93] Lukacs, *HCC*, p. 103.

[94]See Max Horkheimer and Theodor Adorno, "The Culture Industry: Enlightenment as Mass Deception," in *Dialectic of Enlightenment*, trans. John Cummings [New York: Continuum, 1987], pp. 120-187 (hereafter cited as Horkheimer and Adorno, *DOE*).

[95]Although I do want to claim that it is easier to conceive of eliminating bank foreclosures than to conceive of eliminating tornadoes, I do understand that "nature" is often considered as more open to conscious control than is the social world. That is, through scientific and technological advance we can continue to understand and "tame" nature. On this understanding of the world we are more likely to divert tornadoes than bank foreclosures.

[96]"The distinction between a worker faced with a particular machine, the entrepreneur faced with a given type of mechanical development, the technologist faced with technology is purely quantitative; it does not directly entail *any qualitative difference in the structure of consciousness.*" Lukacs, *H&CC*, p. 98. See also pp. 103 - 106.

[97]To understand just how tenuous this objectivity is, suppose the "structurally unemployed" decide to take to the streets and intervene physically in the "objective" discourse about their situation. Then the apparently objectively true "fact" that there need be "structurally unemployed" will be shown to be contextual. Consider also the many late 20$^{th}$ century squatters' movements in Berlin, New York, and Rio where poor and homeless people occupy vacant buildings. The fact that habitable buildings and people with no building to live in both just naturally exist is shattered when people claim the spaces for their own uses. In some of these cases (eg: Thompkins Square Park, NYC, summer 1989) the thin facade of restraint is removed from the face of authority and naked force is used to 'restore order' (i.e.: reassert the primacy of property rights in late capitalism).

[98]Kant wrote a different critique to explain/analyze the role of reason and practical activity in each of these life-spheres: Immanuel Kant, *Critique of Pure Reason*, trans. Norman Kemp Smith [New York: St. Martin's, 1965] -- scientific; Immanuel Kant *Critique of Practical Reason*, trans. Lewis White Beck [Indianapolis, IN: Bobbs-Merrill, 1956] -- ethical; Immanuel Kant, *Critique of Judgment*, [New York: Hafner Press, 1951] -- aesthetic; Immanuel Kant, *Religion Within the Bounds of Reason Alone*, [La Salle, IL: Open Court Publishing, 1960] -- religious. In his neo-Kantian sociology, Weber finds the Kantian distinctions embodied in everyday life in capitalist culture.

[99]Kant, *Critique of Pure Reason*, p. 273.

[100]One of the clearest examples of the cleavages and distance which reified consciousness expresses is found in the practice of social science where the

methodology often requires setting other humans up as objects and fixing their being in order that social relations be captured by quantitative methods.

[101] See Martin Heideggar, *Being and Time*, [New York: Harper and Row, 1962].

[102] Lukacs, *HCC*, p. 145.

[103] Lukacs, *HCC*, p. 145.

[104] Lukacs, *HCC*, p. 110.

[105] Andrew Feenberg, *Lukacs, Marx and the Sources of Critical Theory*, [New York: Oxford University Press, 1986], p. 87.

[106] Lukacs is not alone in this attempt. At roughly the same time Pragmatists such as William James and John Dewey were also attempting to think through this epistemological impasse of modern philosophy. Given this, it is no great surprise that Habermas draws on two other members of the Pragmatists tradition, Charles Sanders Pierce and George Herbert Mead.

[107] Lukacs, *HCC*, p. 148.

[108] Lukacs, *HCC*, p. 170.

[109] Feenberg, *Lukacs, Marx and the Sources of Critical Theory*, p. 125.

[110] Lukacs, *HCC*, p.145.

[111] Lukacs. *HCC*, p. 149.

[112] This seems especially true in the U.S. with its short historical memory as well as its official and publicly expressed belief that anyone can make it "if he works hard enough."

[113] We might also note that there is little consciousness of the historical antecedents of the cultural production of late-capitalism. For example, McDonalds can use a version of Bertold Brecht and Kurt Weill's "Mac the Knife" to sell hamburgers. Apparently no irony was intended. And, Madonna can loosely reconstruct Fritz Lang's *Metropolis* in her video for "Express Yourself." In the latter case it seems likely that Madonna wishes her video to resonate with the echoes of the earlier movie. Although I have made no scientific survey, my experience suggests that very few people in MTV's target

audience catch the reference. The problem is not what Bloom, Hirsch, Bennett and their ilk suggest. The problem is not that one cannot live and function well in the late twentieth century without historical knowledge. No, one can function quite well without the 'burden' of such knowledge. The problem, as I understand it, is that the lack of such knowledge helps legitimate the belief one of my students articulated in class on 9 April 1991, "Capitalism is a natural product of human history. Socialism isn't, it was thought up by many people, not just Marx." The implication being that Capitalism was something we just have to live with because unlike any alternative, Capitalism is not the product of conscious human activity but of an unchanging human nature. The further implication is that a unchanging human nature would take normative precedent over any conscious human activity.

[114] Fredric Jameson, *Marxism and Form: Twentieth Century Dialectical Theories of Literature*, [Princeton, NJ: Princeton University Press, 1971], p. 186.

[115] Lukacs, *HCC*, p. 171.

[116] Lukacs, *HCC*, p. 171.

[117] Lukacs, *HCC*, p. 171.

[118] Lukacs, *HCC*, pp. 21ff.

[119] Lukacs, *HCC*, pp. 186ff.

[120] Lukacs acknowledges the possible fragmentation of proletarian struggle and consciousness. See, *HCC*, pp. 75-77.

[121] Theodor W. Adorno quoted in *The Essential Frankfurt School Reader*, ed. Andrew Arato and Eike Gebhardt [New York: Continuum, 1982], p. 369.

[122] In this essay, I will primarily be concerned with the work of Max Horkheimer, Theodor Adorno and Herbert Marcuse. There have been numerous books and articles published in recent years on the Frankfurt School. Good histories are Helmet Dubiel, *Theory and Politics: Studies in the Development of Critical Theory*, [Cambridge, MA: The MIT Press, 1985]; Rolf Wiggershaus, *The Frankfurt School: Its History, Theories and Political Significance*, [Cambridge, MA: MIT Press, 1994]; and Martin Jay, *The Dialectical Imagination: A History of the Frankfurt School and the Institute of Social Research, 1923-1950*, [Boston: Little Brown, 1973]. A good general introduction is David Held, *Introduction to Critical Theory*, [Berkeley: University of California Press, 1980] and for the connections and discontinuities with post-structuralist thought: Peter Dews, *Logics of*

*Disintegration: Post-Structuralist Thought and the Claims of Critical Theory*, [New York: Verso, 1987].

[123]On 'critical' and 'scientific' Marxism, see Alvin Gouldner, *The Two Marxisms*.

[124]Horkheimer and Adorno, *DOE*, p. 16.

[125]Horkheimer identifies both "Idealism" and "Naturalism" with identity thinking and so both ultimately serve the same purpose. See Max Horkheimer, *The Eclipse of Reason*, [New York: Seabury Press, 1974], p. 170 (hereafter cited as Horkheimer, *EOR*).

[126]Horkheimer, *EOR*, p. 182.

[127]Horkheimer, *EOR*. See also, Horkheimer, "Traditional and Critical Theory" in *Critical Theory*.

[128]Here "instrumental reason" identifies the same tendency that Weber called "formal rationality" and what Marcuse called "technical rationality."

[129]Although Horkheimer takes John Dewey to task for his Naturalism, the account of judging theory which Horkheimer relies upon is remarkably like the pragmatist theory of truth found in Pierce, Dewey and William James. For more on Dewey's instrumentalism see Hickman, *John Dewey's Pragmatic Technology*.

[130]Horkheimer, "Traditional and Critical Theory" in *Critical Theory*, p. 213 (hereafter cited as Horkheimer, "Traditional and Critical Theory").

[131]Horkheimer, "Traditional and Critical Theory," pp. 213-214.

[132]Horkheimer, "Traditional and Critical Theory," p. 214

[133]Theodor Adorno, *Negative Dialectics*, [New York: Seabury, 1979], p. 320.

[134]For more on Hegel's theodicy and its relation to the optimism in Marx and Lukacs see Chapter I.

[135]See, Fredric Jameson, *The Political Unconscious*. pp. 50-53.

[136]Adorno, *Negative Dialectics*, p. 21.

[137] See Simon Schama, *Citizens: A Chronicle of the French Revolution*, [New York: Knopf, 1989]. Schama argues that the French Revolution was really a dispute between those who already had power which got out of hand because the revolution proclaimed ideals which the existing elites were not prepared to realize for all French women and men.

[138] Adorno, *Negative Dialectics*, pp. 20-22.

[139] See Horkheimer and Adorno, *DOE* pp. 43-80.

[140] Particularly helpful on understanding how the rationality of subsystems goes hand in hand with systemic irrationality is the work of Henri Lefebvre. As he argues, the 'technical-bureaucratic society' is strikingly deficient of technicality as a whole. What is sold as 'rational' is in fact "a cover for the obverse." What we get is a series of substitutions: consumer products, such as Tang, as fallout from the space program (or so we were told) instead of a 'rational' technocracy that was itself to stand in for political and economic leadership. Not that we want leaders, but Lefebvre's point, and Horkheimer and Adorno's as well, is that we don't even get that which the existing system holds out as its greatest achievements. We don't even get what we have been promised. See Lefebvre, *Everyday Life in the Modern World* pp. 45-60.

[141] Foucault will make a similar claim in response to questions about his own seemingly seamless and hopeless account of modern life. See Chapter VI.

[142] I will discuss Marcuse on remembrance and the aesthetic later in this chapter. See also Herbert Marcuse, *Eros and Civilization*, [Boston: Beacon Press, 1969].

[143] For a discussion of "capitalism and the authoritarian state" see David Held, *Introduction to Critical Theory*, pp. 52-65.

[144] Theodor Adorno in *The Positivist Dispute in German Sociology*, [New York: Harper and Row, 1976], p. 146.

[145] Horkheimer and Adorno, *DOE*, pp. 83-84.

[146] Horkheimer and Adorno, *DOE*, p. xvi.

[147] Horkheimer and Adorno, *DOE*, p. 25.

[148] Horkheimer and Adorno, *DOE*, pp. 7-8.

[149]See Lucio Colletti, *Marxism and Hegel*, [London: New Left Books, 1973]; Zoltan Tar, *The Frankfurt School: the Critical Theories of Max Horkheimer and Theodor W. Adorno*, [New York: John Wiley, 1977]. In each case, the author interprets Horkheimer and Adorno's critique to be directed solely against quantification and miss the means/ends question.

[150]Horkheimer and Adorno, *DOE*, p. 24.

[151]"State capitalism" is the term coined by Friedrich Pollock to describe the transformed German state and economy under National Socialism. "State Capitalism" is characterized by the state, or bureaucracy, taking over the role of the private capitalist. Used by subsequent theorists to describe the Soviet Union. See Friedrich Pollock, "State Capitalism," *Studies in Philosophy and Social Science* 9, (1941): 201; Friedrich Pollock, "Is National Socialism a New Order?" *Studies in Philosophy and Social Science* 9, (1941): 442-454. See also Max Horkheimer, "The Authoritarian State," *Telos*, no. 15, (Spring 1983); C. L. R. James, *State Capitalism and World Revolution*, [Chicago: Charles H. Kerr Publishing, 1986).

[152]Another analysis of the historical and political situations under Stalin, Hitler and FDR can be found in the work of Mario Tronti and other members of the Italian "Workers power" movement. According to their analysis, the New Deal and the Fordist Compromise represent not the buying off of labor, but one of the greatest victories of labor. Habermas brings back to the Critical Theory tradition the recognition of distinctions of this sort.

[153]Theodor Adorno, *Minima Moralia*, [New York: Verso, 1991], p. 156.

[154]Their arguments against the decaying effects of mass entertainment are strikingly similar to those offered by Rousseau against the theatre. See Jean-Jacques Rousseau, *Politics and the Arts: Letter to D'alembert on the Theatre*, [Ithaca, NY: Cornell University Press, 1960].

[155]For an account of the manner in which new forms of entertainment worked i) to construct a "classless" ideal and identity, and ii) to commodify non-work time see David Nasaw, *Going Out: The Rise and Fall of Public Amusements*, [Basic Books, 1994].

[156]Edward Shils, "Daydreams and Nightmares: Reflections on the Criticism of Mass Culture," *Sewannee Review* 45, (Autumn 1957): 598. In *Late Marxism: Adorno, or, the Persistence of the Dialectic*, [New York: Verso, 1990], Fredric Jameson argues that this sort of critique misses the point of Adorno's critique of mass culture. Jameson argues that Adorno is i) critical of individual works of mass culture, not mass culture as such. And, ii) that Adorno and Horkheimer

understand mass culture as a privileged place of "convergence between monopoly and instrumentalization," because mass culture "can be observed more clearly than other types of commodity exchange" pp. 106-108. On the other h and, J ameson a lso n otes t hat p opular c ulture is excluded, by Adorno, from consideration as art in Theodor Adorno, *Aesthetic Theory*, [Boston: Routledge and Kegen Paul, 1984]. Regardless of whether Horkheimer and Adorno hold an elitist attitude toward mass culture or not, they do often fail to recognize the contradictory moments within mass culture. See Fredric Jameson, "Reification and Utopia in Mass Culture," *Social Text* 1, (Winter 1979): 130-148. See also Chapters V-VII of this work.

[157] Theodor Adorno, *Prisms*, [London: Neville Spearman, 1967], p. 109.

[158] This sort of decision procedure, although I doubt Horkheimer and Adorno would approve of that label, is similar to William James discussion of 'an authentic choice' in "The Will to Believe," in *The Writings of William James*, ed. John J. McDermott, [Chicago: University of Chicago Press, 1967], pp. 717-735. In this piece James argues that often we are faced with a decision situation in which refusing to decide (and act) is to allow the existing trajectory to continue. That is, what appears to be a refusal to choose is in fact a choice for what would happen without our intervention.

[159] For example, Karl Popper, "Reason or Revolution," in *The Positivist Dispute in German Sociology*, [New York: Harper and Row, 1976].

[160] Herbert Marcuse quoted in Alain Martineau, *Herbert Marcuse's Utopia*, [Montreal: Harvest House, 1986], p. 86.

[161] For more on reading Adorno see Fredric Jameson, *Late Marxism: Adorno, or the Persistence of the Dialectic*.

[162] Nancy Fraser, "Struggle over Needs: Outline of a Socialist-Feminist Critical Theory of Late-Capitalist Political Culture," in *Unruly Practices: Power, Discourse and Gender in Contemporary Social Theory*, [Minneapolis: University of Minnesota Press, 1989).

[163] Rick Roderick, *Habermas and the Foundations of Critical Theory*, [MacMillan: London, 1986], p. 40.

[164] Max Horkheimer quoted in *The Essential Frankfurt School Reader*, p. 369.

[165] Horkheimer and Adorno, *DOE*, Introduction and Chapter 1.

[166] Max Horkheimer, "The Latest Attack on Metaphysics," in *Critical Theory*, pp. 132-187.

[167] This sort of mechanistic optimism is, as we've noted, one way to read Marx. Such a position in clearly expressed by Engels in Friedrich Engels. *Anti-Duhring*, [Moscow: Foreign Languages Publishing House, 1962].

[168] Horkheimer and Adorno, *DOE*, p. xii.

[169] Horkheimer and Adorno, *DOE*, p. 118.

[170] Horkheimer, "The Latest Attack on Metaphysics," p. 158.

[171] Horkheimer, "The Latest Attack on Metaphysics," pp. 158-159.

[172] Note once again a striking parallel to the pragmatist account of knowledge as a relation found in the work of William James and John Dewey.

[173] In this critique Horkheimer and Adorno replicate arguments made by Edmund Husserl, *The Crisis of European Sciences and Transcendental Phenomonology: An Introduction to Phenomenological Philosophy*, trans. David Carr [Evanston, IL: Northwestern University Press, 1970]. See, Horkheimer and Adorno, *DOE*, pp. 24-25 and Horkheimer "The Latest Attack on Metaphysics," pp. 146-147n. Habermas is concerned to examine the role of the idea of "objectivity" in modern science, see Chapter III of this work.

[174] Horkheimer, "The Latest Attack on Metaphysics," p. 154.

[175] See Theodor Adorno, "Sociology and Empirical Research" in *The Positivist Dispute in German Sociology*.

[176] Horkheimer and Adorno, *DOE*, p. 28.

[177] Adorno, "Sociology and Empirical Research", p. 69.

[178] Herbert Marcuse, *Reason and Revolution*, [Boston: Beacon Press, 1960], p. 341 (hereafter cited as Marcuse, *RAR*).

[179] Marcuse, *RAR*, p. 343.

[180] Marcuse, *RAR*, pp. 323-388.

[181] Lezsek Kolawoski identifies three characteristics of utopian faith. They are:
  i) the belief that we can control our future,
  ii) the idea that effective theory and action toward a future under our control do exist, and

iii) the conviction that we can understand the dereified (i.e.: 'true') character of our present existence. Cited in Alain Martineau, *Herbert Marcuse's Utopia*, [Montreal: Harvest House, 1986], pp. 4-5. For some additional thinking on the utopian moment see Ernst Bloch, *The Principle of Hope*, 3 vols, [Cambridge, MA: MIT Press, 1986], Paul Ricoeur, "The Task of the Political Educator," *Philosophy Today* 17, (Summer 1973): 140-152, Tom Moylan, *Imagine the Impossible: Science Fiction and the Utopian Imagination*, [New York: Methuen, 1986], Erin McKenna, *The Task of Utopia*, [Lanham, MD: Roman and Littlefield, 2002].

[182] Herbert Marcuse, *One-Dimensional Man: Studies in the Ideology of Advanced Industrial Society*, [Boston: Beacon Press, 1968], pp. 7-8 (hereafter cited as Marcuse, *ODM*).

[183] My reading of Marcuse owes much to the work of Douglas Kellner, especially his book *Herbert Marcuse and the Crisis of Marxism*, [Berkeley: University of California Press, 1984].

[184] Herbert Marcuse, "Some Social Implications of Modern Technology" in *The Essential Frankfurt School Reader*, ed. Andrew Arato and Eike Gebhart [New York: Continuum, 1990], pp. 138-162 (hereafter cited as Marcuse, "Some Social . . .").

[185] Marcuse, "Some Social . . . ," pp. 138-142.

[186] Marcuse, "Some Social . . . ," p. 146.

[187] Marcuse, "Some Social . . . ," pp. 149-154.

[188] At least in such works as we have extant. Marx claimed that his planned book on the state was the one book that he alone could write. Unless his conception of the state was radically unlike that indicated by the trajectory of his existing writings, this would have contained some analysis of ideology.

[189] See, Hans Magnus Enzenberger, *The Consciousness Industry*, [New York: Seabury, 1974]

[190] Marcuse, *ODM*, p. xiv.

[191] Marcuse, *ODM*, p. xv.

[192] For instance, in the passage just cited Marcuse continues:

> The first tendency is dominant, and whatever preconditions for a reversal may exist are being used to prevent it. Perhaps an accident may alter the

situation, but unless the recognition of what is being done and what is being prevented subverts the consciousness and the behavior of man, not even a catastrophe will bring about the change. Marcuse, *ODM*. p. xv.

[193]Marcuse, *ODM*, p. 223, and 256-257. See also, Herbert Marcuse, *An Essay on Liberation*, [Boston: Beacon Press, 1969], and Herbert Marcuse, *The Aesthetic Dimension*, [Boston: Beacon Press, 1978].

[194]Herbert Marcuse, "Philosophy and Critical Theory," in *Negations*, [Boston: Beacon Press, 1968], p. 142.

[195]Marcuse, *ODM*, p. ix.

[196]This move also functions to make it more difficult to locate responsibility. The individual capitalist might be held accountable and might even feel obligated to engage in certain projects in the public interest (ex. Carnegie), but corporations follow a different logic, that of profit. Witness how even 'progressive' corporations such as Ben and Jerry's decide the best way to change the system is to follow its logic and thus i) also follow profit logic and ii) have a vested interest in the preservation of the system.

[197]This process leads to increasing rates of surplus value that furthers the concentration of capital. See Paul Baran and Paul Sweezy, *Monopoly Capital*, [New York: Monthly Review Press, 1966]; Harry Braverman, *Labor and Monopoly Capital*, [New York: Monthly Review Press, 1974].

[198]On the history and theories of management since the mid-10th Century see Stephan P. Waring, *Taylorism Transformed: Scientific Management Theory Since 1945*, [Chapel Hill, NC: University of North Carolina Press, 1991].

[199]Marcuse, *ODM*, p. 9.

[200]Marcuse, *ODM*, pp. 11-12.

[201]From a Foucauldian perspective, Zygmunt Bauman argues that jogging, healthfoods, the natural foods craze, and the new abstinence are all new modes of disciplinary power which construct bodies and individuals in the interests of capitalism. See Bauman, "Industrialism, Consumerism, and Power," in *Theory, Culture and Society* 1, (1983): 32-43. Also, many feminists have discussed the social construction of bodies and needs. See Susan Bordo, "Anorexia Nervosa: Pschopathology as the Crystallization of Culture," *The Philosophical Forum* 27, (Winter 1985-86): 73-104; Donna Haraway, "A Manifesto for Cyborgs: Science, Technology, and Socialist Feminism in the 1980s" in *Feminism/Postmodernism* ed. Linda J. Nicholson [New York: Routledge,

1990], pp. 190-233; Elizabeth Spellman, *Inessential Women: Problems of Exclusion in Feminist Thought*, [Boston: Beacon Press, 1988]; Susan Rubin Suleiman, ed., *The Female Body in Western Culture: Contemporary Perspectives*, [Cambridge, MA: Harvard University Press, 1986].

[202] Marcuse, *ODM*, pp. 4-5.

[203] For example, Merry-Go-Round, a clothing store, used to advertise that it sold individuality at over 400 stores coast to coast.

[204] Douglas Kellner, *Critical Theory, Marxism, and Modernity*, [Baltimore: Johns Hopkins University Press, 1989], p. 160.

[205] See Stanley Aronowitz, *False Promises*, [New York: McGraw Hill, 1973].

[206] Marcuse, *ODM* p. 6.

[207] Marcuse, *ODM*, pp. 6-7.

[208] Perry Anderson, *Considerations on Western Marxism*, [New York: Verso, 1987]. p. 83.

[209] Stanley Aronowitz, *False Promises*, [New York: McGraw Hill, 1973]. This sort of account is also absent from most of Horkheimer and Adorno's work.

[210] See Kellner, *Herbert Marcuse and the Crisis of Marxism*.

[211] Herbert Marcuse, *Counterrevolution and Revolt*, [Boston: Beacon Press, 1972], pp. 18ff.

[212] In *Situationists International Anthology*, ed. Ken Knapp, [Berkeley: Bureau of Public Secrets, 1981], p. 6.

[213] Marcuse, *ODM*, p. 256.

[214] See "Theory and Politics: A Discussion with Herbert Marcuse, Jürgen Habermas, Heinz Lubasz and Telman Spengler," *Telos* 11, (Winter 1978-79): 150-152. Also, Herbert Marcuse, "Protosocialism and Late Capitalism: Toward a Theoretical Synthesis Based on Bahro's Analysis," in *Rudolph Bahro: Critical Responses*, edited by, Ulf Walter, [White Plains, NY: M. E. Sharpe, Inc, 1980], pp. 25-48 (hereafter cited as Marcuse, "Protosocialism").

[215] Marcuse, *An Essay on Liberation*, pp. 52-54.

[216] Marcuse, *An Essay on Liberation*, p. 79.

[217] Herbert Marcuse, "Revolutionary Subject and Self Government," Praxis 5, (1969): 326.

[218] See Marcuse, *ODM*, pp. 66-71. In these pages Marcuse discusses Brecht's notion of the "estrangement effect."

[219] Marcuse, *ODM*, p. 39.

[220] Marcuse, "Protosocialism," p. 32.

[221] Stanley Aronowitz in a presentation to the Radical Scholars and Activists' Conference in Chicago, October 1990. See also Kellner, *Critical Theory, Marxism and Modernity*, pp. 152-166.

[222] On the contradictory moments in consumer culture see Kellner, *Critical Theory, Marxism and Modernity*, pp. 152-166. On the aesthetic possibility of everyday life see John Dewey, *Art as Experience*, [New York: Peregee Books, 1980]. See also Chapters V-VII of this work.

[223] Marcuse, *Counterrevolution and Revolt*, p. 121. See also Marcuse, *ODM*, p. 248.

[224] See Christopher Lasch, *The Culture of Narcissism*, [New York: Warner Books, 1979]. Also, for a discussion of this trend in the 1980s see Chapters V-VII below.

[225] Jürgen Habermas, *Autonomy and Solidarity*, [London: Verso, 1986], p. 182. For the best introduction of Habermas early work to the English speaking world see Thomas McCarthy, *The Critical Theory of Jürgen Habermas* [Cambridge, MA: MIT Press, 1978] My own reading owes much to Rick Roderick, *Habermas and the Foundations of Critical Theory*, [London: Macmillan, 1986]. See also, Martin Beck Matustik, *Jürgen Habermas: A Philosophical-Political Profile*, [New York: Rowman and Littlefield, 2001].

[226] Martin Jay, *Marxism and Totality: The Adventures of a Concept from Lukacs to Habermas*, [Berkeley: University of California Press, 1984], pp. 462-463.

[227] Jürgen Habermas, "Between Philosophy and Science: Marxism as Critique," in *Theory and Practice*, [Boston: Beacon Press, 1973], p. 235 (hereafter cited as Habermas, *TAP*).

[228] Jürgen Habermas, "A Reply to my Critics", in *Habermas: Critical Debates*, ed. John B. Thompson and David Held, [Cambridge, MA: MIT Press, 1982], p. 238.

[229] Jürgen Habermas, *Communication and the Evolution of Society*, [Boston: Beacon Press, 1979], p. 95.

[230] Jürgen Habermas, "Between Philosophy and Science: Marxism as Critique", in *TAP*, p. 198. Two comments on this passage are in order. First, Habermas continues "Especially in the form codified by Stalin." This would seem to excuse Western Marxism from the point. Yet, as he points out, the reaction to Marxism in general is today shaped by these facts. Second, in the German these facts are characterized as "four facts against Marx." See "Zwischen Philosophie und Wissenschaft. Marxismus als Kritik" in *Theorie und Praxis*, [Berlin: Neuwied, 1967], pp. 228-290.

[231] Habermas, *TAP*, pp. 195-196. As is increasingly clear, to claim that conditions such as hunger (where hunger = lack of food to eat) no longer exist in advanced capitalist society is to offer, at best, only a partial truth. In this country alone the past 15 years have been witness to an increasing number of people with no home and not enough food to eat. Of course, the fact that few laugh or cry when a president claims, as did Ronald Reagan, that these people choose to live this way is but further evidence of the power of ideology to obscure even the most obvious truths. Habermas, of course, knows this and is attempting to identify forces other than straightforward economic forces that might limit the acceptance of Marxism, in any form.

[232] Habermas, *TAP*, p. 196.

[233] Habermas, *TAP*, p. 196.

[234] Habermas, *TAP*, p. 169.

[235] See Karl Marx, *Grundrisse*, [New York: Vintage, 1973].

[236] Habermas, "Between Philosophy and Science," pp. 195-252.

[237] This can lead to violent repression in the name of advancing socialism. Such occurrences are not rare. The explanation that deviations from the true revolutionary socialist path must be crushed has been used to justify these state interventions in popular movements: Hungary, 1956; Prague, 1968; Beijing, 1989; Lithuania, 1991; and others.

[238] Jürgen Habermas, *Toward a Rational Society*, [Boston: Beacon Press, 1970], p. 113 (hereafter cited as Habermas, *TRS*).

²³⁹Habermas, *TRS*, pp. 112-113. He can also be read as arguing that new sorts of people, new forms of subjectivity are necessary. See Martin Matustik, *Postnational Identity*.

²⁴⁰Jürgen Habermas, *Knowledge and Human Interest*, [Boston: Beacon, 1971], p. vii (hereafter cited as Habermas, *KHI*).

²⁴¹Habermas, *KHI*, pp. 43-65.

²⁴²This understanding of knowledge as a function of human activity is quite similar to that of John Dewey. Dewey locates knowledge as only one of the many ways we transact with the world and grapple with the problems that we confront.

²⁴³Habermas, *KHI*, p. 194.

²⁴⁴In "Labor and Interaction," Habermas discusses Hegel's conception of Spirit as a product of human interaction formed through three media: i) symbolic representation, ii) labor (or control of nature), and iii) interaction (or struggle for recognition). According to Habermas, Marx, and Hegelian Marxists, have collapsed these three media into labor. Habermas' initial move is to reintroduce interaction. See, Jürgen Habermas, "Labor and Interaction," in *TAP*, pp. 140ff. In *KHI* Habermas expands this account to include an emancipatory interest.

²⁴⁵Habermas, *KHI*, pp. 301-317.

²⁴⁶Habermas, *KHI*, p. 43.

²⁴⁷Habermas, *KHI*, p. 195.

²⁴⁸*Habermas, KHI*, p. 309.

²⁴⁹Karl-Otto Apel, "The a priori of Communication and the Foundation of the Humanities", *Man and World*, no.5, (1972), p. 10.

²⁵⁰Thomas McCarthy, *The Critical Theory of Jürgen Habermas*, [Cambridge, MA: MIT Press, 1978], p. 7.

²⁵¹See Thomas Kuhn, *The Structure of Scientific Revolutions*, [Chicago: University of Chicago Press, 1970]. See also Gwen. A. Pearson, "A Funny Thing Happened on the Way to Graduate School," *American Entomologist* (forthcoming); Sandra Harding, *The Science Question in Feminism*, [Ithaca, NY: Cornell University Press, 1986); Helen Longino, *Science as Social*

*Knowledge: Values and Objectivity in Scientific Inquiry*, Princeton, NJ: Princeton University Press, 1990]; Andrea Nye, *Words of Power: A Feminist Reading of the History of Logic*, [New York: Routledge, 1990].

[252] See Jürgen Habermas, "Technological Progress and the Social Life-World" in *Towards a Rational Society*, pp. 50-61.

[253] Habermas, *KHI*, p. 195.

[254] Habermas, *KHI*, p. 195.

[255] Habermas, *KHI*, p. 140.

[256] Habermas, *KHI*, p. 155.

[257] Habermas, *KHI*, p. 310.

[258] Habermas, *KHI*, p. 310.

[259] Habermas, *KHI*, p. 309.

[260] See Hans-Georg Gadamer, *Truth and Method*, [London: Sheed and Ward, 1975].

[261] Jürgen Habermas, "Summation and Response", *Continuum* 8, (Summer 1970): 125.

[262] Gadamer responds with an oft-heard critique of Critical Theory. He argues that Habermas is privileging the critic's point of view and encouraging an elitist refusal to enter into debate and dialogue with others who hold different opinions/speak a 'different language'. See "The Scope and Function of Hermeneutical Reflection," in *Philosophical Hermeneutics*, ed. D. Linge, [Berkeley: University of California Press, 1976]. In response we should note that on occasion the refusal to enter into existing discourse relations can be an effective strategy against oppression and can direct challenges to the dominant discourse can transform that discourse. For example: the success of the women's movement in translating 'wife beating' into 'wife battering' with its connotations of punishable violence. Or, consider the partial success of ACT-UP, and other AIDS activists to transform the public debate around AIDS policy around the world. See also David Ingram, "Habermas, Gadamer, and Bourdieu on Discourse: A Communication Ethic Reconsidered," *Man and World*, no. 15, (1982), pp. 149-161.

[263] Jürgen Habermas, *TAP*, pp. 22-23.

[264] Theodor W. Adorno, "Sociology and Psychology," *New Left Review*, no. 47, (1968).

[265] See Herbert Marcuse, *Eros and Civilization*, [Boston: Beacon Press, 1969].

[266] Habermas, *KHI*, p. 214.

[267] Habermas, *KHI*, pp. 266-269.

[268] Habermas, *KHI*, p. 276.

[269] Habermas, *KHI*, p. 288. See also, Sigmund Freud, *Civilization and Its Discontents*.

[270] Held, *Introduction to Critical Theory*, p. 277.

[271] Bill Martin, "The Enlightenment's Talking Cure: Habermas, *Legitimation Crisis*, and the Recent Political Landscape," *Southwest Philosophy Review* 4, (January 1988): 33-44.

[272] For a version of this sort of critique see Martin Jay, *Marxism and Totality* [Berkeley: University of California Press, 1984], pp. 480ff.

[273] See Michel Foucault, *Madness and Civilization* [New York: Pantheon, 1965]. Also, *Discipline and Punish*, [New York: Vintage Books, 1979], and *The History of Sexuality, vol. I.*, [New York: Vintage Books, 1980]. I am grateful to David Shumway for bringing this line of discussion to my attention. For further discussion of Foucault see David Shumway, *Michel Foucault*, [Boston: Twayne Publishers, 1989]. See also Chapters VI and VII.

[274] For a discussion of democracy, discourse ethics, and the concrete demands often only implicit in Habermas' work see David Ingram, *Philosophy and Critical Theory*, [New York: Paragon House, 1990], pp. 146-151.

[275] Habermas, *TRS*, pp. 107-109.

[276] See Habermas, *TRS*, and Jürgen Habermas, *The Structural Transformation of the Public Sphere: An Inquiry into a Category of Bourgeois Society*, trans. Thomas Burger [Cambridge, MA: MIT Press, 1989] (hereafter cited as Habermas, *Public Sphere*).

[277] David Held, "Crisis Tendencies, Legitiation and the State," in *Habermas and Modernity*, ed. Richard Berstein, [Cambridge, MA: MIT Press, 1985], p. 181.

[278] See Habermas, *TAP*, and Jürgen Habermas, *Legitimation Crisis*, trans. Thomas McCarthy [Boston: Beacon Press, 1975].

[279] The claim that oppression has taken on a less economic character is only true if we ignore the global nature of capitalism and the privileged situation of those of us who live in the 'First World'. Even in the U.S. this claim is not true in relative terms, and might be false in absolute terms over the past 13 years. See Kevin Phillips, *The Politics of Rich and Poor: Wealth and the American Electorate in the Reagan Aftermath*. [New York: Random House, 1990] See also "The Concentration of Wealth in the United States" [Washington, D.C.: Joint Economic Committee, United States Congress, 1986]; and Donald L. Barlett and James B. Steele, *America: What Went Wrong?* [Kansas City: Andrews and McMeel, 1992]. I am grateful to Judith Bradford for bringing this last work to my attention.

[280] Habermas, *Legitimation Crisis*, p. 39. This is one of the passages in which Habermas clearly locates his work within the Marxist tradition.

[281] Habermas, *Legitimation Crisis*, p. 92.

[282] For example, most public discourse about the U.S. recessions in the early 1980s and early 1990s framed the problem in terms of failed economic policy. 'Economic policy' means the management decisions made by political leaders after they determine the most rational manner to achieve continued economic growth. What failed and caused these recessions is not the economy itself, rather the failure was one of management (or congress, or the president). Similarly, the October 1987 stockmarket crash was written off to a variety of causes, including computer driven trading (talk about fetishizing technology), but seldom was the crash analyzed in relation to underlying economic factors such as declining productive capacity in the U.S., the decline in well-paying manufacturing jobs and concomitant declining consumer purchasing power. See Barlett and Steele, *America: What Went Wrong?*.

[283] For example, the mid-April 1991 rail workers' strike in the U.S. One of the few possible means to advance workers' interests is to stop work. In this case the political managers of 'our' economy ordered the workers back to work within 24 hours of the beginning of the strike. The justification was 'national economic interest'. A similar situation occurred in the late 1980s United Mine Workers' strike against Pittston coal. The miners were 'allowed' to strike. At the same time they were under a court order not to interfere with continued production. In each case the interests of the striking workers was dismissed in favor of the corporate interest in continued profit. This dismissal was justified as necessary for 'the national interest' (i.e.: necessary for the preservation of the existing political and economic orders) without a national discussion about our interests in this matter.

[284]For a discussion of the construction of national and special interests and how this distinction works to legitimate business as usual, see Iris Marion Young, "Polity and Group Difference: A Critique of the Ideal of Universal Citizenship," in *Feminism and Political Theory*, ed. Cass R. Sunstein, [Chicago: University of Chicago Press, 1990]. pp. 117-141.

[285]See Daniel Hellinger and Dennis R. Judd, *The Democratic Facade*, Second Edition, [Belmont, CA: Wadsworth Publishing Company, 1994]. Hellinger and Judd develop an argument along these lines intended to show that the United States has been in a legitimation crisis since the 1980s. While their argument reads a bit much like a conscious conspiracy tale for my taste, and they do not make reference to the Habermasian position, this is an informative book. I am greatful to Kara Sweeney for bring this work to my attention.

[286]A clear example of this is repeated resistance to voter registration drives. One possible reason, even if never consciously articulated, is that voter registration drives not only register those who dislike the national administration, such drives also register people who often find local party organizations and officials unreceptive to their needs and ideas. Many local party organizations find their power challenged by the newly registered, or active, voters. Furthermore, many of the new voters and activists were likely to support the more 'liberal' and least 'practical' (i.e.: 'rational') candidates. Opening existing structures to more participation and debate can be detrimental to the continued existence of those structures, or at least to the continued dominance of those presently in power. On those who choose to and choose not to vote, see Phillips, *The Politics of Rich and Poor*. On the language used to discredit the Jesse Jackson voter registration campaign in 1988, see Susan J. Douglas, ""Time" does Jackson in with Subliminal Message," *In These Times*, (April 20-26, 1988): 16.

[287]See Jürgen Habermas, "Towards a Theory of Communicative Competence," *Inquiry* 13, (1970): 368-372. See also, Jürgen Habermas, "On Systematically Distorted Communication," *Inquiry* 13, (1970): 205-218. For a more detailed account of the relation between Habermas' work on speech act theory and universal pragmatics, and the work of Noam Chomsky, J.L. Austin, and John Searle, see Roderick, *Habermas and the Foundations of Critical Theory*, pp. 73-100.

[288]Habermas, *Legitimation Crisis*, pp. 110-113.

[289]Habermas, *Communication and the Evolution of Society*, pp. 1-6.

[290]Habermas, *Communication and the Evolution of Society*, pp. 45-68. See also John B. Thompson, "Universal Pragmatics" in *Habermas: Critical Debates*.

[291]See Kant, *Groundwork of the Metaphysics of Morals*.

[292]The phrase 'October Surprise' refers to alleged activities on behalf of the 1980 Reagan/Bush election campaign to undermine President Carter's attempts to gain the release of U.S. citizens held as hostages in Iran. See Gary Sick, "The Election Story of the Decade," The New York Times, 15 April 1991, p. A17. See also, Christopher Hitchens, "Minority Report" *The Nation* 252, (April 22, 1991): 511; Robert Morris, "Behind the 'October Surprise'" *The Village Voice* 36, (May 21, 1991): 31-35; PBS, "Frontline," April 16, 1991, "The Election Held Hostage."

[293]For example, in 1984 polls indicated that many voters disagreed with Ronald Reagan's stance on domestic issues but voted for him nonetheless. Their decision was certainly based on factors other than the force of the better argument, factors such as patriotism, insecurity, xenophobia, and memory (or lack thereof).

[294]Habermas, *Legitimation Crisis*, pp. 48-49, and 69-84.

[295]Habermas, Jürgen, *Autonomy and Solidarity*, ed. Peter Dews [London: Verso, 1986], p. 109 (hereafter cited as Habermas, *A&S*).

[296]On cultural parallels see Raymond Williams on "homology," in *Marxism and Literature*, [Oxford: Oxford University Press, 1977], pp. 101-108.

[297]See Jürgen Habermas, *The Philosophical Discourse of Modernity*, [Cambridge, MA: MIT Press, 1987] (hereafter cited as Habermas, *PDM*).

[298]Here I am following the account of modernity formulated by the 'Budapest School'. See Ferenc Feher, Agnes Heller and Gyorgy Markus, *Dictatorship over Needs*, [Oxford: Basil Blackwell, 1983].

[299]See John F. Rundell, *Origins of Modernity: The Origins of Modern Social Theory from Kant to Hegel to Marx*, [Cambridge: Polity Press, 1987].

[300]See Jürgen Habermas, *The Theory of Communicative Action*, 2 vols, trans Thomas McCarthy [Boston: Beacon Press, 1984-1987] (hereafter cited as Habermas *TCA*). In this essay I focus on Volume 2. For more extended commentary on Volume 1 see Rick Roderick, *Habermas and The Foundations of Critical Theory*. See also David Ingram, *Habermas and the Dialectic of Reason*, [New Haven: Yale University Press, 1987].

[301] By "stock of meanings" I intend the sociological usage and refer to those things which we must 'know' in order to play the roles we play everyday. For example, through our years in school we learn that it is inappropriate to have a "secret word" (borrowed from "Pee Wee's Playhouse") in a university philosophy class. That is, we find that at some point we can act in appropriate ways for the student or professor role.

[302] Habermas, *TCA*, 2:119-140.

[303] Habermas, *TCA*, 2:143-145.

[304] Habermas, *A&S*, pp. 108-109.

[305] Habermas, *TCA*, 2:143-145.

[306] Habermas, *TCA*, 2:145-148. Also, *TCA*, 1:157-158.

[307] Habermas, *TCA*, 2:27-42. Many objections have been raised to Kohlberg's account of moral-cognitive development. Along with these objections have come criticisms of Habermas' use of Kohlberg's theory. See Carol Gilligan, *In A Different Voice*, [Cambridge, MA: Harvard University Press, 1982]. Also, Seyla Benhabib, "The Generalized and the Concrete Other: The Kohlberg-Gilligan Controversy and Feminist Theory," in *Feminism and Critique: On the Politics of Gender* ed. Seyla Benhabib and Drucilla Cornell, [Minneapolis: University of Minnesota Press, 1987].

[308] Habermas, *TCA*, 2:77-118.

[309] Habermas, *TCA*, 2:148-149.

[310] See my discussions of Hegel, Lukacs and the dialectic in Chapter 1.

[311] Habermas, *TCA*, 2:150.

[312] Habermas, *TCA*, 2:150.

[313] Habermas, *TCA*, 1:229ff and 340-344. Also, Habermas, *TCA*, 2:302-332.

[314] Habermas, TCA, 2:172-178.

[315] I am grateful to Rick Roderick for suggesting this line of discussion. See Habermas, *TRS*, and Chapter VI of this essay for further discussion of this topic.

[316] Habermas, *TCA*, 2:153.

[317] This process was traced in detail by Habermas in *Legitimation Crisis*.

[318] Habermas, *TCA*, 2:153-165.

[319] Habermas, *TCA*, 2:179.

[320] Habermas, *TCA*, 2:168-173.

[321] Habermas, *Legitimation Crisis*, pp. 19-23. See also Marx's discussion of the seeming freedom of exchange relations under capitalism in *Capital*, Vol.1.

[322] Habermas, *TCA*, 2:186.

[323] Habermas, *TCA*, 2:271

[324] Niklas Luhmann, *The Differentiation of Society*, [New York: Columbia University Press, 1982], pp. 150-175. Luhmann seems relatively content with the cybernatized system he describes. In many ways his discussion of the social system is similar to Baudrillard's account of contemporary society, especially in *America* [New York: Verso, 1988]. Unlike Luhmann, Baudrillard may still be seeking a way out.

[325] In recent years much has been made in the United States of "total quality management" -- an idea which claims to emphasize employee involvement in decisions and to "empower" employees. These programs are usually instituted by management and may work to lessen the subjective experience of alienation while leaving the objective conditions intact. See Tom Juravich, *Chaos on the Shop Floor: A Worker's View of Quality, Productivity, and Management*, [Philadelphia: Temple University Press, 1985].

[326] Habermas, *TCA*, 2:181-185.

[327] See my discussion of Bourdieu's notion of cultural capital in Chapter V for a clarification and expansion of Habermas' account of economic capital (money) and political capital (power).

[328] Habermas, *TCA*, 2:182-185 and 270-282.

[329] As evidence we find the class of experts who regularly appear on television news programs telling us what to think about various events in the world. One of the primary sources of legitimation for these talking heads is an advanced degree and a university or think-tank job. See Alexander Cockburn, "The

Tedium Twins," in *Corruptions of Empire: Life Studies and the Reagan Era*, [New York: Verso, 1987], pp. 199-206.

[330] Habermas, *TCA*, 2:184-186, 200-210, 318-319, and 346-347. See the work of Baudrillard for further discussion of the role of the mass media in late capitalist society

[331] See Chapter VI of this essay and Nancy Fraser, *Unruly Practices* [Minneapolis: University of Minnesota Press, 1989].

[332] Jürgen Habermas, "New Social Movements," *Telos*, no. 49, (Fall 1991), p. 33. For a survey of recent sociological literature on the new social movements see *New Social Movements: From Ideology to Identity*, [Philadelphia: Temple University Press, 1994]. Most of the work in this volume argues against the continued use of "class" as a helpful concept. For a more activist and politically engaged response see Carl Boggs, *Social Movements and Political Power: Emerging Forms of Radicalism in the West*, [Philadelphia: Temple University Press, 1986].

[333] Habermas, *TCA*, 2:356-360.

[334] Habermas, *TCA*, 2:367-373.

[335] *David Ingram, Habermas and the Dialectic of Reason*, [New Haven: Yale University Press, 1987], p. 161.

[336] Habermas, *TCA*, 2:360-364.

[337] Habermas, *TCA*, 2:285-299.

[338] Habermas, *TCA*, 2:179-195, 283-300.

[339] For example: the German Social Democratic Party in the early 20th century, or the British Labour Party for much of its history.

[340] Habermas, "New Social Movements," pp. 33-37.

[341] Habermas, *TCA*, 2:302-331.

[342] This is a significant move for Habermas as his ideal speech situation appeared to speak for all. In arguing for the ideal speech situation Habermas seemed to be proposing a theory of an abstract general human interest in emancipation. At this point, he seems to be describing emancipatory interests that are formed in the ongoing process of everyday living. These interests

contain within them a universalizing thrust that could be revolutionary. Here is the possible moment of thinking totality, thinking beyond the local, which can draw attention toward the necessity of systemic change.

[343] Habermas, *PDM*, p. 365.

[344] Habermas, *TCA*, 2:395-396.

[345] Stephen White, *The Recent Work of Jürgen Habermas*, [New York: Cambridge University Press, 1988], p. 125.

[346] Habermas, *PDM*, p. 364.

[347] Habermas, *A&S*, p. 198.

[348] Habermas, *TAP*, p. 196.

[349] See Marx *Capital*, vol. 1, pp. 505-506, 579-580, 777-781, and 920ff. Marx argues that one effect of moving to an international credit economy is to further mask primitive accumulation. A primary economic tool that moves this process is international debt. See also, Karl Marx, *Grundrisse*, [New York: Vintage Books, 1973], p. 535. Also, Karl Marx, *Capital*, volume 3, [New York: Vintage Books, 1981], p. 612.

[350] E. P. Thompson, *The Making of the English Working Class*, [New York: Vintage, 1966]. p. 11.

[351] For more on the formation of class and class consciousness through shared lived experiences see: Herbert G. Gutman, *Power and Culture: Essays on the American Working Class*, [New York: Pantheon, 1987].

[352] Habermas, *TAP*, p. 197. This has long been a tension within Marxism -- the relation between the objective and subjective aspects of experience/facts about the world. See my discussion of Lukacs in Chapter 1. See also a discussion of the subjective experience as alienating and proletarian in Garsons, *The Electronic Sweatshop*.

[353] See James O'Connor, "Capital, Crisis, Class Struggle," in *Rethinking Marxism: Struggles in Marxist Theory*, edited by, Stephen Resnick and Richard Wolff, [Brooklyn, NY: Autonomedia, 1985]. O'Connor suggests an even stronger reading of Habermas at this point. O'Connor writes, "According to Habermas, crises do not exist unless they are subjectively experienced," p. 287.

[354] James O'Connor, "Capital, Crisis, Class Struggle," pp. 273-293.

³⁵⁵Consider the racist and homophobic screeds of Guns 'n' Roses on *G 'n' R Lies*, or more recently the lyrics of the rapper Eminem. Many rock critics interpreted these lyrics as authentic and justified, although misdirected, expressions of what it meant to be a working class white male with few employment prospects.

³⁵⁶Gabriel Ixmata, "Testimony of Gabriel Ixmata," in *Guatemala on Trial*, edited by Susanne Jonas, Ed McCaughen and Elizabeth Sutherland Martinez, [San Francisco: Synthesis Publications, 1984]. I am grateful to John Hibbitts for bringing this text to my attention.

³⁵⁷For more on the 'gift' of work see Baudrillard..

³⁵⁸Staughton Lynd, "Youngstown, Ohio: Rebuilding the Labor Movement from Below," in *Fire in the Hearth: The Radical Politics of Place in America*, edited by Mike Davis, Steven Hiatt, Marie Kennedy, Susan Riddick and Micheal Sprinker, [New York: Verso, 1990], pp. 177-194.

³⁵⁹Lynd, "Youngstown, Ohio," p. 193.

³⁶⁰Richard Sennett and Jonathan Cobb, *The Hidden Injuries of Class*, [New York: Vintage, 1972], p. 9.

³⁶¹Goodwyn also uncovered a cultural condescension toward workers and working class language during his investigation of Solidarity. Goodwyn, ""Consciousness" and the Language of Social Analysis." See also Judith Bradford, "Discourses of Prostitution," [unpublished manuscript]. She argues that experts who are experientially outside a certain cultural space are legitimated to talk about it, but those who are (or remain) within are discounted as not having appropriate distance and self-understanding.

³⁶²I discuss the accusations that Habermas' work is the 'ideology of the new class' later in this chapter.

³⁶³See Seyla Benhabib, *Critique Norm and Utopia: A Study in the Foundations of Critical Theory*, [New York: Columbia University Press, 1986].

³⁶⁴Nancy Fraser, "Struggle over Needs," p. 163.

³⁶⁵See Chapter IV.

³⁶⁶Seyla Benhabib, "The Generalized and the Concrete Other." See also, Iris Marion Young, "Polity and Group Difference: A Critique of the Ideal of Universal Citizenship," in *Feminism and Political Theory*, ed. by Cass R.

Sunstein, [Chicago: University of Chicago Press, 1990], pp. 117-141, Carole Pateman, *The Sexual Contract*, [Stanford, CA, Stanford University Press, 1988], Tamsin Lorriane, *Gender, Identity, and The Production of* Meaning, [Boulder, CO: Westview Press, 1991], Patrica J. Huntington, *Ecstatic Subjects, Utopia, and Recognition : Kristeva, Heidegger, Irigaray,* [Albany, NY: SUNY Press, 1998], and Susan J. Hekman, *Gender and Knowledge: Elements of a Postmodern Feminism*, [Boston: Northeastern University Press, 1990].

[367] Benhabib, "The Generalized and the Concrete Other," p. 87

[368] Benhabib, "The Generalized and the Concrete Other," p. 87.

[369] Benhabib, "The Generalized and the Concrete Other," p. 87.

[370] Nancy Fraser, "What's Critical about Critical Theory: The Case of Habermas and Gender," in *Unruly Practices*, pp. 113-143.

[371] Young, "Polity and Group Difference," p. 121.

[372] Habermas, *TCA*, 2:93-394.

[373] See Fraser, "What's Critical about Critical Theory."

[374] Hekman, *Gender and Knowledge*, p. 162.

[375] Carole Pateman, *Participation and Democratic Theory*, [Cambridge: Cambridge University Press, 1970]; Jane Mansbridge, *Beyond Adversarial Democracy*, [New York: Basic Books, 1980]; Amy Gutmann, *Liberal Democracy,* [Cambridge: Cambridge University Press, 1980]. For some further reflections on identity and politics, see William Wilkerson and Jeffrey Paris, *New Critical Theory: Essays on Liberation*, [Lanham, MD: Rowman and Littlefield, 2001] and Jacqueline M. Martinez, *Phenomenology of Chicana Experience and Identity*, [Lanham, MD: Rowman and Littlefield, 2001].

[376] Pierre Bourdieu, "Artistic Taste and Cultural Capital," in *Culture and Society: Contemporary Debates*, ed. Jeffery C. Alexander and Steven Seidman, [Cambridge: Cambridge University Press, 1990], pp. 205-213; Pierre Bourdieu, *Distinction*, [Cambridge, MA: Harvard University Press, 1986]. For a different sort of critique of the rather arid cultural landscape reflected in Habermas' work, see Alison Leigh Brown, *Fear, Truth, and Writing: From Paper Village to Electronic Community* [Albany, NY: SUNY Press, 1995].

[377] Bourdieu, "Artistic Taste and Cultural Capital," p. 212.

[378]The process of resacralization demonstrates capitalism's ability to recoup the liberatory possibilities of its own histories. In "The Work of Art in the Age of Mechanical Reproduction," (In *Illuminations*, [New York: Shoken Books, 1969]), Walter Benjamin argues that new technologies mean the death of the aura of 'authentic' art. He further argues that this process has liberatory potentials. Following Benjamin, John Berger notes in *Ways of Seeing*, [London: BBC and Penguin Books, 1972] that by the late 20$^{th}$ century:
> Very few people are aware of what has happened because the means of reproduction are used nearly all the time to promote the illusion that nothing has changed except that the masses, thanks to reproduction, can now begin to appreciate art as the cultured minorities once did. pp. 32 - 33.

[379]Bourdieu, "Artistic Taste and Cultural Capital," p. 213.

[380]In an effort to avoid sexual discrimination lawsuits, many companies have set up programs designed to introduce women to the cultural norms of corporate life, including where and with whom to play golf or racquetball. No overturning of the norms here, but at least a recognition that 'objective' standards do serve to exclude some people.

[381]One need only think of the family values debate, from Dan Quayle to the Gingrich inspired "Contract with America". This last contains language clearly designed to define a "normal" way of living and proposes a legislative program designed to encourage this sort of life.

[382]Habermas, *TCA*, 2:393-403.

[383] See Cornelis Disco, "Critical Theory as the Ideology of the New Class," *Theory and Society* 8, (1979): 159-214.

[384]Alvin Gouldner, *The Future of Intellectuals and the Rise of the New* Class, [New York: Seabury, 1979].

[385]Disco, "Critical Theory as the Ideology of the New Class," p. 190.

[386]Henning Ottmann, "Cognitive Interests and Self-Reflection" in *Habermas: Critical Debates*, edited by John B. Thompson and David Held, [Cambridge, MA: MIT Press, 1982], p. 96.

[387]This description was suggested by Rick Roderick during a discussion of Habermas, new social movements, coalitions, and the prospects for political change during the 1990s.

[388] Dieter Misgeld, "Critical Hermeneutics vs NeoParsonianism," *New German Critique* 35, (Spring/Summer 1985): 60.

[389] At the same time, I would argue that some theory is necessary. Or, at least can be useful. See chapter VI.

[390] Paulo Friere, *Pedagogy of the Oppressed*, [New York: Continuum, 1983], p. 58.

[391] Habermas, *TAP*, p. 40.

[392] Friere, *Pedagogy of the Oppressed*, p. 33.

[393] Thomas McCarthy, "Complexity and Democracy, or the Seducements of Systems Theory," *New German Critique* 35, (Spring/Summer 1985): 53.

[394] See Jacques Ellul, *The Technological Society*, trans. John Wilkinson [New York: Vintage Books, 1964].

[395] Habermas, *A&S*, p. 187.

[396] See Habermas, *Public Sphere*.

[397] Nancy Fraser, "Rethinking the Public Sphere: A Contribution to the Critique of Actually Existing Democracy," in *Habermas and the Public Sphere*, edited by Craig Calhoun, [Boston: MIT Press, 1991]. I am grateful to Nancy Fraser for allowing me access to the prepublication manuscript of this essay. Page references are to the manuscript.

[398] Fraser, "Rethinking the Public Sphere," p. 29.

[399] James O'Connor, *Accumulation Crisis*, [New York: Oxford University Press, 1984]; William Greider, *Secrets of the Temple: How the Federal Reserve Rune the Country*, [New York: Simon and Schuster, 1987]; Claus Offe, *Disorganized Capitalism: Contemporary Transformations of Work and Politics*, [Cambridge, MA: MIT Press, 1985]; Claus Offe, *Contradictions of the Welfare State*, [Cambridge, MA: MIT Press, 1984].

[400] On what it means to be able to get there from here, when an alternative social arrangement is an option, see Bernard Williams, "The Truth in Relativism" in *Moral Luck*, [Cambridge: Cambridge University Press, 1981].

[401] Fredric Jameson, *Late Marxism: Adorno, or, the Persistence of the Dialectic*, [New York: Verso, 1990].

[402] Habermas, *A&S*, p. 152.

[403] Habermas, *A&S*, p. 146.

[404] Michel Foucault, *Power/Knowledge: Selected Interviews & Other Writings, 1972-1977*, ed. Colin Gordon, [New York: Pantheon Books, 1980], p. 159 (hereafter cited as Foucault, *Power/Knowledge*).

[405] The reading I develop here is, I think, warranted by Foucault's texts. Nonetheless, there are attempts to read Foucault as developing a non-normative "ethics." See Romand Coles, *Self/Power/Other: Political Theory and Dialogic Ethics*, [Ithaca, NY: Cornell University Press, 1992]; and Axel Honneth, *The Critique of Power: Reflective Stages in a Critical Theory of Power*, [Cambridge, MA: MIT Press, 1991].

[406] Foucault, *Power/Knowledge*, pp. 38-39, 104-105, 158-159.

[407] Michel Foucault, *Discipline and Punish: The Birth of the Prison*, [New York: Vintage Books, 1979], p. 202 (hereafter cited as Foucault, *D&P*).

[408] Michel Foucault, *The Birth of the Clinic: An Archeology of Medical Perception*, [New York: Vintage, 1975], p. 28 (hereafter cited as Foucault, *BOC*).

[409] Foucault, *D&P*, pp. 202-203.

[410] Foucault, *Power/Knowledge*, pp. 152-153.

[411] Foucault, *Power/Knowledge*, p. 208.

[412] Foucault, *HOS*, p. 93.

[413] Nancy Fraser, *Unruly Practices: Power Discourse and Gender in Contemporary Social Theory*, [Minneapolis, University of Minnesota Press, 1989], p. 59.

[414] See Foucault, *HOS*, p. 96.

[415] Habermas, *PDM*, pp. 283-284.

[416] Habermas, *A&S*, p. 211.

[417] See Goodwyn, ""Consciousness" and the Language of Social Analysis."

[418] Gilles Delueze and Felix Guattari, *Anti-Oedipus: Capitalism and Schizophrenia*, [Minneapolis: University of Minnesota Press, 1983].

[419] Henri Lefebvre, *Everyday Life in the Modern World*; Guy Debord, *The Society of the Spectacle*; Raoul Vaneigem, *The Book of Pleasures*, [London: Pending Press, 1983].

[420] Especially Dewey, *Art as Experience*; and parts of John McDermott, *Streams of Experience*.

[421] Jacques Derrida, *Limited, Inc.*, and *Margins of Philosophy*, trans. Alan Bass [Chicago: University of Chicago Press, 1982]; Michael Ryan, *Politics and Culture: Working Hypotheses for a Post-Revolutionary Society*.

[422] In the United States there is a new generation of critical social theorists who are at work thinking through the possibilities of a politically engaged critical theory at the beginning of the century. These thinkers include some who have influenced my own thinking: Judith Bradford, Alison Brown, Patricia Huntington, Tamsin Lorraine, Bill Martin, Martin Matustik, William Wilkerson, Erin McKenna, and George Trey.

[423] Habermas, *A&S*, P. 187.

[424] See chapters IV and VI.

[425] See Habermas, *TCA*, 2:434.

[426] Habermas, *A&S*, p. 187.

[427] Raymond Williams, "Towards Many Socialisms," in *Resources of Hope: Culture, Democracy, Socialism*, [New York: Verso, 1989], p. 295.

[428] Williams, "Towards Many Socialisms," pp. 295-296.

[429] Billy Bragg, "North Sea Bubble," from the CD *Don't Try This at Home*, New York: Elektra Entertainment, 1991.

[430] Williams, "Towards Many Socialisms," p. 297.

[431] Richard Rorty, *Contingency, Irony, and Solidarity*, [New York: Cambridge University Press, 1989], pp. 67-69 (hereafter cited as Rorty, *CIS*).

[432] This might, in some sense, be true. Of course, the truth of the convergence thesis is an empirical question. See Doug Ireland, "More You Watch, Less You Know," *The Village Voice* 36, (March 5, 1991): 8. Ireland cites a study

conducted at the University of Massachusetts that surveyed the relation between knowledge and attitudes toward the 1990-1991 (so far) Persian Gulf War. The survey determined, interestingly enough, those who knew only the administration line supported the war. Those who knew additional information (about the US ambassador or that Israel occupies Arab lands) were likely to be skeptical or opposed. So, actually knowing stuff **might**, in some circumstances, lead people to similar beliefs.

[433] Rorty, *CIS*, p. xvi. The "[s]" is my addition. If I am correct in my argument, then "freedom" will have multiple meanings in the future just as it has in the past and has it does now. I think that if we take Rorty's arguments in this book seriously, then one implication of his position, regardless of whether we agree with his arguments (and I think he is dangerously wrong in places), is that freedom must have multiple meanings in a democracy. On the problematic political implications, because of the lack of historical consciousness, of irony see also Franco Moretti, "The Spell of Indecision" *New Left Review*, no. 164, (July/August 1987), pp. 34-43.

# SELECTED BIBLIOGRAPHY

Adorno, Theodor W. *Aesthetic Theory*. Boston: Routledge and Kegen Paul, 1984.
    *Minima Moralia*. New York: Verso, 1991.
    *Negative Dialectics*. New York: Seabury, 1979.
    *Prisms*. London: Neville Spearman, 1967.
    "Sociology and Psychology." *New Left Review*, no. 47, (1968). in *The Essential Frankfurt School Reader*, p. 369. Edited by Andrew Arato and Eike Gebhardt. New York: Continuum, 1982.
Adorno, Theodor, et al. *The Positivist Dispute in German Sociology*. New York: Harper and Row, 1976.
Althusser, Louis. *Reading Capital*. London: New Left Books, 1970.
    "Ideology and Ideological State Apparatuses." In *Lenin and Philosophy*. New York: Monthly Review Press, 1971.
Anderson, Perry. *Considerations on Western Marxism*. London: Verso, 1979.
Apel, Karl-Otto. "The a priori of Communication and the Foundation of the Humanities." *Man and World*, no.5, (1972), p. 10.
Aronowitz, Stanley. *The Crisis in Historical Materialism: Class, Politics and Culture in Marxist Theory*. 2nd ed. Forward by Colin MacCabe. Minneapolis: University of Minnesota Press, 1990.
    *False Promises*. New York: McGraw Hill, 1973.
    "The Future of Socialism?" *Social Text*, no. 24, (1990), pp. 85-116.
Bagdikian, Ben H. "The Lords of the Global Village." In *The Nation* 450 (June 12, 1989): 805 - 820.
Baran, Paul and Sweezy, Paul. *Monopoly Capital*. New York: Monthly Review Press, 1966.
Barlett, Donald L. and James B. Steele, *America: What Went Wrong?*. Kansas City: Andrews and McMeel, 1992.
Bauman, Zygmunt. "Industrialism, Consumerism, and Power." *Theory, Culture and Society* 1 (1983): 32-43.
Baynes, Kenneth. *The Normative Grounds of Social Criticism*, Albany, NY: SUNY Press, 1992.
Beiner, Ronald. *Philosophyin a Time of Lost Spirit*. Toronto: University of Tornoto Press, 1997.
Benhabib, Seyla, *Critique Norm and Utopia: A Study in the Foundations of Critical Theory*. New York: Columbia University Press, 1986.
    "The Generalized and the Concrete Other: The Kohlberg-Gilligan Controversy and Feminist Theory." In *Feminism and Critique: On the Politics of Gender*. Edited by Seyla Benhabib and Drucilla Cornell. Minneapolis: University of Minnesota Press, 1987.
Benjamin, Walter. "The Work of Art in the Age of Mechanical Reproduction." In *Illuminations*. Edited and with an Introduction by Hannah Arendt. New York: Schocken Books, 1969.
Berger, John. *Ways of Seeing*. London, BBC and Penguin Books, 1972.

Bernal, Martin. *Black Athena.* New Brunswick, NJ: Rutgers University Press, 1987. Vol. 1: *The Fabrication of Ancient Greece, 1785-1985.*
Best, Steve. "The Commodification of Reality and the Reality of Commodification." *Current Perspectives In Social Theory* 9 (1987): 37.
"Marx and the Problem of Conflicting Models of History." *The Philosophical Forum* 22 (Winter 1990): 167-192.
Bloch, Ernst. *The Principle of Hope.* 3 vols. Cambridge, MA: MIT Press, 1986.
Boggs, Carl. *Social Movements and Political Power: Emerging Forms of Radicalism in the West.* Philadelphia: Temple University Press, 1986.
Bookchin, Murray. *The Ecology of Freedom: The Emergence and Dissolution of Hierarchy.* Palo Alto, CA: Cheshire Books, 1985.
Bordo, Susan. "Anorexia Nervosa: Pschopathology as the Crystallization of Culture." *The Philosophical Forum* 27 (Winter 1985-86): 73-104.
Bourdieu, Pierre. *Distinction.* Cambridge, MA: Harvard University Press, 1986.
"Artistic Taste and Cultural Capital." In *Culture and Society: Contemporary Debates.* Edited by Jeffery C. Alexander and Steven Seidman. Cambridge: Cambridge University Press, 1990.
Braaten, Jane, *Hamermas' Critical Theory of Society.* Albany, NY: SUNY Press, 1991.
Braverman, Harry. *Labor and Monopoly Capital.* New York: Monthly Review Press, 1974.
Brown, Alison Leigh. *Fear, Truth, and Writing: From Paper Village to Electronic Community* Albany, NY: SUNY Press, 1995.
Buraway, Michael. "Marxism is Dead, Long Live Marxism!" *Socialist Review* 20 (April/June 1990): 7-19.
Camus, Albert. *The Myth of Sisyphus and Other Essays.* New York: Vintage Books, 1955
Castells, Manuel. *High Technology, Space and Society.* Beverly Hills, CA: Sage Publications, 1985.
Cleaver, Harry. "Karl Marx: Economist or Revolutionary?" *In Marx, Schumpter and Keynes: A Centenary Celebration of Dissent.* Edited by Suzanne W. Helburn and David F. Bramhall. Armonk: M. E. Sharpe, 1986.
Cockburn, Alexander. "The Tedium Twins." In *Corruptions of Empire: Life Studies and the Reagan Era.* New York: Verso, 1987.
Cohen, G. A. *Karl Marx's Theory of History: A Defence* Oxford: Clarendon Press, 1978.
Coles, Romand. *Self/Power/Other: Political Theory and Dialogical Ethics.* Ithaca, NY: Cornell University Press, 1992.
Colletti, Lucio. *Marxism and Hegel.* London: New Left Books, 1973.
Culler, Jonathan. *On Deconstruction.* Ithaca: Cornell University Press, 1982.
Delueze, Gilles and Guattari, Felix. *Anti-Oedipus: Capitalism and Schizophrenia.* Minneapolis: University of Minnesota Press, 1983.
Debord, Guy. *The Society of the Spectacle.* Detroit: Black and Red, 1970.

de Man, Paul. *Blindness and Insight: Essays in the Rhetoric of Contemporary Criticism*. London: Methuen, 1983.
Derrida, Jacques. *Specters of Marx*. New York: Routledge, 1994.
*Limited Inc.* Evanston, IL: Northwestern University Press, 1988.
*Margins of Philosophy*. Translated by Alan Bass. Chicago: University of Chicago Press, 1982.
*Positions*. Chicago: University of Chicago, 1981.
Devall, Bill and Sessions, George. *Deep Ecology: Living as if Nature Mattered*. Salt Lake City: Peregrine Smith Books, 1985.
Dewey, John. *Art as Experience*. New York: Peregee Books, 1980.
Dews, Peter. *The Limits of Disenchantment*. New York: Verso, 1995.
*Logics of Disintegration: Post-Structuralist Thought and the Claims of Critical Theory*. New York: Verso, 1987.
Dienstag, Joshua Foa. *Dancing in Chains*. Stanford, CA: Stanford, 1997.
Disco, Cornelis. "Critical Theory as the Ideology of the New Class." *Theory and Society* 8 (1979): 159-214.
Douglas, Susan J. ""Time" does Jackson in with Subliminal Message." *In These Times*, (April 20-26, 1988): 16.
Dubiel, Helmut. *Theory and Politics: Studies in the Development of Critical Theory*. Cambridge, MA: MIT Press, 1985.
Dunn, Charles J. "Jailing the Unnaceptable." *The Raleigh (North Carolina) News and Observer*, Sunday, April 21, 1991, p. 7J.
Ellul, Jacques. *The Technological Society*. Translated by John Wilkinson. New York: Vintage Books, 1964.
Engels, Friedrich. *Anti-Duhring*. Moscow: Foreign Languages Publishing House, 1962.
Enzenberger, Hans Magnus. *The Consciousness Industry*. New York: Seabury, 1974.
Feenberg, Andrew. *Lukacs, Marx and the Sources of Critical Theory*. New York: Oxford University Press, 1986.
*Critical Theory of Technology*. New York: Oxford University Press, 1991.
Feher, Ferenc.; Heller, Agnes Heller.; and Markus, Gyorgy. *Dictatorship over Needs*. Oxford: Basil Blackwell, 1983.
Feuerbach, Ludwig. *Essence of Christianity*. New York: Harper and Row, 1957.
*Principles of the Philosophy of the Future*. Indianapolis, IN: Hackett, 1986.
Foucault, Michel. *Archeology of Knowledge*. New York: Pantheon Books, 1972.
*The Birth of the Clinic: An Archeology of Medical Perception*. New York: Vintage, 1975.
*Discipline and Punish*. New York: Vintage Books, 1979.
*The History of Sexuality*. Vol. I. New York: Vintage Books, 1980.
*Madness and Civilization*. New York: Pantheon, 1965.

*Power/Knowledge: Selected Interviews & Other Writings, 1972-1977.*
Edited by Colin Gordon. New York: Pantheon Books, 1980.

Fraser, Nancy. *Unruly Practices: Power Discourse and Gender in Contemporary Social Theory.* Minneapolis, University of Minnesota Press, 1989.

"Rethinking the Public Sphere: A Contribution to the Critique of Actually Existing Democracy." In *Habermas and the Public Sphere.* Edited by Craig Calhoun. Boston: MIT Press, 1991.

Friere, Paulo. *Pedegogy of the Oppressed.* New York: Continuum, 1983.

Fukuyama, Francis. "The End of History?" *The National Interest.* (Summer 1989).

Gadamer, Hans-Georg Gadamer. *Truth and Method.* London: Sheed and Ward, 1975.

"The Scope and Function of Hermeneutical Reflection." In *Philosophical Hermeneutics.* Edited by D. Linge. Berkeley: University of California Press, 1976.

Garson, Barbara. *The Electronic Sweatshop: How Computers are Transforming the Office of the Future into the Factory of the Past.* New York: Penguin Books, 1988.

Gideon, Siegfried. *Mechanization Takes Command: A Contribution to Anonymous History.* New York: Oxford University Press, 1948.

Gilligan, Carol. *In A Different Voice.* Cambridge, MA: Harvard University Press, 1982.

Goodwyn, Larry. ""Consciousness" and the Language of Social Analysis: The Awkward Conjunction of Poland and the West," presented to the Duke University Marxism and Society Program, October 1988.

Gottdeiner, Mark. *The Social Production of Urban Space.* Austin: University of Texas Press, 1985.

Greider, William. *Secrets of the Temple: How the Federal Reserve Runs the Country.* New York: Simon and Schuster, 1987.

Gouldner, Alvin. *The Future of Intellectuals and the Rise of the New Class.* New York: Seabury, 1979.

*The Two Marxisms.* New York: Seabury Press, 1980

Gutman, Herbert G. *Power and Culture: Essays on the American Working Class.* New York: Pantheon, 1987.

Gutmann, Amy. *Liberal Democracy.* Cambridge: Cambridge University Press, 1980.

Habermas, Jürgen. *Autonomy and Solidarity.* London: Verso, 1986.

*Communication and the Evolution of Society.* Boston: Beacon Press, 1979.

*The Inclusion of the Other.* Cambridge, MA: The MIT Press, 1998.

*Justification and Application.* Cambridge, MA: The MIT Press, 1993.

*Knowledge and Human Interest.* Boston: Beacon, 1971.

*Legitimation Crisis.* Translated by Thomas McCarthy. Boston: Beacon Press, 1975.

*Moral Consciousness and Communicative Action.* Cambridge, MA: The MIT Press, 1990.
*The Past as Future.* Lincoln: University of Nebraska Press, 1994.
*The Philosophical Discourse of Modernity.* Cambridge, MA: MIT Press, 1987.
*The Structural Transformation of the Public Sphere: An Inquiry into a Category of Bourgeois Society.* Translated by Thomas Burger. Cambridge, MA: MIT Press, 1989.
*Theorie und Praxis.* Berlin: Neuwied, 1967.
*Theory and Practice.* Boston: Beacon Press, 1973.
*The Theory of Communicative Action.* 2 vols. Translated by Thomas McCarthy Boston: Beacon Press, 1984-1987.
*Toward a Rational Society.* Boston: Beacon Press, 1970.
"New Social Movements." *Telos*, no. 49, (Fall 1981), p. 33.
"On Systematically Distorted Communication." *Inquiry* 13, (1970): 205-218.
"A Reply to my Critics." In *Habermas: Critical Debates.* Edited by John B. Thompson and David Held. Cambridge, MA: MIT Press, 1982.
"Summation and Response." *Continuum* 8 (Summer 1970): 125.
"Towards a Theory of Communicative Competence." *Inquiry* 13 (1970): 368-372.
Harding, Sandra. *The Science Question in Feminism.* Ithaca, NY: Cornell University Press, 1986.
Haraway, Donna. "A Manifesto for Cyborgs: Science, Technology, and Socialist Feminism in the 1980s." In *Feminism/Postmodernism.* Edited by Linda J. Nicholson. New York: Routledge, 1990.
Hegel, G. W. F. *Logic.* New York: Oxford University Press, 1982.
*Phenomonology of Spirit.* Translated by A. V. Miller. New York: Oxford University Press, 1977.
*The Philosophy of History.* New York: Dover Publications, 1956.
*The Philosophy of Right.* New York: Oxford University Press, 1967.
Hekman, Susan J. *Gender and Knowledge: Elements of a Postmodern Feminism.* Boston: Northeastern University Press, 1990.
Held, David. *Introduction to Critical Theory.* Berkeley: University of California Press, 1980.
"Crisis Tendencies, Legitimation and the State." In *Habermas and Modernity.* Edited by Richard Berstein. Cambridge, MA: MIT Press, 1985.
Hellinger, Daniel and Dennis R. Judd. *The Democratic Facade.* Belmont, CA: Wadsworth Publishing Company, 1994.
Hickman, Larry. *John Dewey's Pragmatic Technology.* Indianapolis, IN: Indiana University Press, 1990.
Hitchens, Christopher. "Minority Report." *The Nation* 252 (April 22, 1991): 511.

Honneth, Axel. *The Critique of Power: Reflective Stages in a Critical Social Theory.* Cambridge, MA: MIT Press, 1991.
hooks, bell. "Talking Back." In *Discourse* 8, (1986): 126.
Horkheimer, Max. "Traditional and Critical Theory." In *Critical Theory: Selected Essays.* Translated by Matthew J. O'Connell. New York: Herder and Herder, 1972.
    *The Eclipse of Reason.* New York: Seabury Press, 1974.
    "The Authoritarian State." *Telos*, no. 15, (Spring 1983).
Horkheimer, Max and Adorno, Theodor. *Dialectic of Enlightenment.* Translated by John Cummings. New York: Continuum, 1987.
Husserl, Edmund. *The Crisis of European Sciences and Transcendental Phenomonology: An Introduction to Phenomenological Philosophy.* Translated by David Carr. Evanston, IL: Northwestern University Press, 1970.
Ingram, David. *Habermas and the Dialectic of Reason.* New Haven: Yale University Press, 1987.
    *Critical Theory and Philosophy.* New York: Paragon House, 1990.
    "Habermas, Gadamer, and Bourdieu on Discourse: A Communication Ethic Reconsidered." *Man and World*, no. 15, (1982), pp. 149-161.
Ireland, Doug. "More You Watch, Less You Know." *The Village Voice* 36 (March 5, 1991): 8.
Ixmata, Gabriel "Testimony of Gabriel Ixmata." In *Guatemala on Trial*, Edited by Susanne Jonas, Ed McCaughen and Elizabeth Sutherland Martinez. San Francisco: Synthesis Publications, 1984.
James, William. "The Will to Believe," In *The Writings of William James.* Edited by John J. McDermott. Chicago: University of Chicago Press, 1967.
Jameson, Fredric. *Late Marxism: Adorno, or, the Persistence of the Dialectic.* New York: Verso, 1990.
    *Marxism and Form: Twentieth Century Dialectical Theories of Literature.* Princeton, NJ: Princeton University Press, 1971.
    *The Political Unconscious.* Ithaca, NY: Cornell University Press, 1981.
    "Postmodernism and Consumer Society." In *The Anti-Aesthetic.* Edited by Hal Foster. Port Townsend, WA: Bay Press, 1983.
    "Postmodernism, or The Cultural Logic of Late Capitalism." *New Left Review*, no. 146, (1984), pp. 52-92.
    "Reification and Utopia in Mass Culture." *Social Text* 1 (Winter 1979): 130-148.
Jay, Martin. *The Dialectical Imagination: A History of the Frankfurt School and the Insitute of Social Research, 1923-1950.* Boston: Little Brown, 1973.
    *Marxism and Totality: The Adventures of a Concept from Lukacs to Habermas.* Berkeley: University of California Press, 1984.
    "The Frankfurt School in Exile." *Perspectives in American History* 6 (1972): 340,

Kant, Immanuel. *Critique of Pure Reason*. Translated by Norman Kemp Smith. New York: St. Martin's, 1965.
   *Groundwork of the Metaphysic of Morals*. Translated by H. J. Paton. New York: Harper Torchbooks, 1956.
   "What is Enlightenment." In *Kant Selections*. Edited by Lewis White Beck. New York: Macmillan, 1988.
Kellner, Douglas, *Critical Theory, Marxism, and Modernity*. Baltimore: Johns Hopkins University Press, 1989.
   *Herbert Marcuse and the Crisis of Marxism*. Berkeley: University of California Press, 1984.
   *Jean Baudrillard: From Marxism to Postmodernism and Beyond*. Cambridge: Polity Press, 1989.
   *Television and the Crisis of Democracy*. Boulder, CO: Westview Press, 1990.
Kellner, Douglas and Roderick, Rick. "Recent Literature on Critical Theory." *New German Critique* 23. (1981): 159-166.
Kelly, Michael. *Hermeneutics and Critical Theory in Ethics*, Cambridge, MA: The MIT Press, 1990.
Knapp, Ken, ed. *Situationist International Anthology*. Berkeley, CA: Bureau of Public Secrets, 1981.
Kojev, Alexandre. *Introduction a la lecture de Hegel; lecons sur La phenomenologie de l'esprit, professees de 1933 a 1939 a l'Ecole des hautes-etudes*. Paris: Gallimard, 1947.
Korsch, Karl. In *Karl Korsch: Revolutionary Theory*. Edited by Douglas Kellner. Austin: University of Texas Press, 1977.
Larana, Enrique, Hanks Johnston and Joseph R. Gusfield, editors. *New Social Movements: From Ideology to Identity*. Philadelphia: Temple University Press, 1994].
Lasch, Christopher. *The Culture of Narcissism*. New York: Warner Books, 1979.
Lazere, Donald., ed. *American Media and Mass Culture*. Berkeley: University of California Press, 1987.
Lefebvre, Henri. *Introduction to Modernity*. New York: Verso, 1995.
   *Everyday Life in the Modern World*. Translated by Sacha Rabinovitch. New Brunswick, NJ: Transaction Books, 1984.
Lenin, Vladimir. "The Three Sources and Component Parts of Marxism." In *Historical Materialism* by Vladimir Lenin, Karl Marx, and Friedrich Engels. Moscow: Progress Publishers, 1970.
Levidow, W. and Robins, Les. *Cyborg Worlds: The Military Information Society*. London: Free Association Books, 1989.
Lorraine, Tamsin. "Postmodern Strategies for Feminist Change." presented to the RPA, Chicago, 1990.
Luhmann, Niklas. *The Differentiation of Society*. New York: Columbia University Press, 1982.

Lukacs, Georg. *History and Class Consciousness.* Cambridge, MA: MIT Press, 1971.
Lynd, Staughton. "Youngstown, Ohio: Rebuilding the Labor Movement from Below." In *Fire in the Hearth: The Radical Politics of Place in America.* Edited by Mike Davis, Steven Hiatt, Marie Kennedy, Susan Riddick and Micheal Sprinker. New York: Verso, 1990.
McCarthy, Thomas. *The Critical Theory of Jürgen Habermas.* Cambridge, MA: MIT Press, 1978.
 "Complexity and Democracy, or the Seducements of Systems Theory." *New German Critique* 35, (Spring/Summer 1985): 53.
MacGregor, David. *The Communist Ideal in Hegel and Marx.* Buffalo: University of Toronto Press, 1984.
MacIntyre, Alasdair. *A Short History of Ethics.* New York: The Macmillan Company, 1971.
Mandel, Ernst. *Late Capitalism.* London: New Left Books, 1975.
Mansbridge, Jane. *Beyond Adversarial Democracy.* New York: Basic Books, 1980.
Marcus, Greil. *Lipstick Traces.* Cambridge, MA: Harvard University Press, 1989. 47.
Marcuse, Herbert. *The Aesthetic Dimension.* Boston: Beacon Press, 1978.
 *Counterrevolution and Revolt.* Boston: Beacon Press, 1972.
 *Eros and Civilization.* Boston: Beacon Press, 1969.
 *An Essay on Liberation.* Boston: Beacon Press, 1969.
 *Negations.* Boston: Beacon Press, 1968.
 *One-Dimensional Man: Studies in the Ideology of Advanced Industrial Society.* Boston: Beacon Press, 1968.
 *Reason and Revolution.* Boston: Beacon Press, 1960.
 "Protosocialism and Late Capitalism: Toward a Theoretical Synthesis Based on Bahro's Analysis." In *Rudolph Bahro: Critical Responses.* Edited by, Ulf Walter. White Plains, NY: M. E. Sharpe, Inc, 1980.
 "Revolutionary Subject and Self Government." *Praxis* 5 (1969): 326.
 "Some Implications of Modern Technology." In *The Essential Frankfurt School Reader.* Edited by Andrew Arato and Eike Gebhart. New York: Continuum, 1990.
Marcuse, Herbert, et al. "Theory and Politics: A Discussion with Herbert Marcuse, Jürgen Habermas, Heinz Lubasz and Telman Spengler." *Telos* 11 (Winter 1978-79): 150-152.
Margalit, Avisai. *The Decent Society.* Cambridge, MA: Harvard, 1996.
Marsh, James L. *Critique, Action, and Liberation.* Albany, NY: SUNY Press, 1995.
Martin, Bill. "The Enlightenment's Talking Cure: Habermas, *Legitimation Crisis,* and the Recent Political Landscape." *Southwest Philosophy Review* 4 (January 1988): 33-44.
 *Matrix and Line.* Albany: State University of New York Press, 1993.
 *THE Radical Project: Sartrean Investigations,* Lanham, MD: Rowman and Littlefield, 2000.

# Bibliography

Martineau, Alain. *Herbert Marcuse's Utopia*. Montreal: Harvest House, 1986.
Martinez, Jacqueline M. *Phenomenology of Chicana Experience and Identity*, Lanham, MD: Rowman and Littlefield, 2001.
Marx, Karl. *Capital. vol. I: A Critique of Political Economy*. Translated by Ben Fowkes. New York: Vintage, 1977.
———. *Capital*. vol. 3. New York: Vintage Books, 1981.
———. *Grundrisse*. New York: Vintage, 1973.
———. *Economic and Philosophic Manuscripts of 1844*. New York: International Publishers, 1964.
———. *The German Ideology*. In *Karl Marx: Selected Writings*. Moscow: Progress Publishers, 1964.
———. "Preface to *A Critique of Political Economy*." In *Karl Marx: Selected Writings*. Edited by David McLellan. New York: Oxford University Press, 1977.
———. "Theses on Feuerbach." In *Marx: Selected Writings*. Edited by David McLellan. New York: Oxford University Press, 1987.
Marx, Karl and Engels, Friedrich. *The Communist Manifesto. in Karl Marx: Selected Writings*. Edited by David McLellan. [New York: Oxford University Press, 1977.
Matustik, Martin. *Postnational Identity: Critical Theory and Existential Philosophy in Habermas, Kierkegaard, and Havel* New York: The Guilford Press, 1993.
McKenna, Erin. *The Task of Utopia*, Lanham, MD: Roman and Littlefield, 2002.
Merleau-Ponty, Maurice. *Adventures of the Dialectic*. Evanston: Northwestern University Press, 1973.
Misgeld, Dieter. "Critical Hermeneutics vs NeoParsonianism." *New German Critique* 35 (Spring/Summer 1985): 60.
Mitzman, Arthur. *The Iron Cage: An Historical Interpretation of Max Weber*. New York: Grosset and Dunlap, 1969.
Moretti, Franco. "The Spell of Indecision." *New Left Review*, no. 164, (July/August 1987).
Morris, Robert. "Behind the 'October Surprise'." *The Village Voice* 36 (May 21, 1991): 31-35.
Moylan, Tom. *Demand the Impossible: Science Fiction and the Utopian Imagination*. New York: Methuen, 1986.
Nasaw, David. *Going Out: The Rise and Fall of Public Amusements*. New York: Basic Books, 1994.
Negri, Toni. "Postscript, 1990." In *Communists Like Us*, by Felix Guattari and Toni Negri, Translated by Michael Ryan New York: Semiotext(e), 1990.
Nye, Andrea. *Words of Power: A Feminist Reading of the History of Logic*. New York: Routledge, 1990.
Park, Shelley and LaRocque, Michelle. "What's a Nice Girl Like Me Doing in a Profession Like This." *Signs* (forthcoming)

O'Connor, James. *Accumulation Crisis.* New York: Oxford University Press, 1984.
"Capital, Crisis, Class Struggle." In *Rethinking Marxism: Struggles in Marxist Theory.* Edited by, Stephen Resnick and Richard Wolff. Brooklyn, NY: Autonomedia, 1985.
Offe, Claus. *Contradictions of the Welfare State.* Cambridge, MA: MIT Press, 1984.
*Disorganized Capitalism: Contemporary Transformations of Work and Politics.* Cambridge, MA: MIT Press, 1985.
Ottmann, Henning. "Cognitive Interests and Self-Reflection." In *Habermas: Critical Debates.* Edited by John B. Thompson and David Held. Cambridge, MA: MIT Press, 1982.
Pateman, Carole. *Participation and Democratic Theory.* Cambridge: Cambridge University Press, 1970.
*The Sexual Contract.* Stanford, CA, Stanford University Press, 1988.
PBS, "Frontline," April 16, 1991, "The Election Held Hostage."
Pearson, Gwen A. "A Funny Thing Happened on the Way to Graduate School." *American Entomologist* (forthcoming).
Phillips, Kevin. *The Politics of Rich and Poor: Wealth and the American Electorate in the Reagan Aftermath.* New York: Random House, 1990.
Pollock, Friedrich. "Is National Socialism a New Order?" *Studies in Philosophy and Social Science* 9 (1941): 442-454.
"State Capitalism." *Studies in Philosophy and Social Science* 9 (1941): 201.
Popper, Karl. *The Open Society and Its Enemies.* Princeton, NJ: Princeton University Press, 1966.
"Reason or Revolution." *In The Positivist Dispute in German Sociology.* New York: Harper and Row, 1976.
Radical Science Collective. *Making Waves: The Politics of Communication.* London: Free Association Books, 1984.
Rasmussen, David M. *Reading Habermas.*, Cambridge MA: Basil Blackwell, 1990.
Regan, Tom. *The Case for Animal Rights.* Berkeley: University of California Press, 1983.
Ricoeur, Paul. "The Task of the Political Educator." *Philosophy Today* 17 (Summer 1973): 140-152.
Roderick, Rick. *Habermas and the Foundations of Critical Theory.* MacMillan: London, 1986.
"Marxism and Philosophy." presented to the Philosophy Department, Duke University, February 1985.
Rorty, Richard. *Contingency, Irony, and Solidarity.* New York: Cambridge University Press, 1989.
Ross, Andrew. *The Chicago Gangster Theory of Life: Nature's Debt to Society.* New York: Verso, 1994.

Rundell, John F. *Origins of Modernity: The Origins of Modern Social Theory from Kant to Hegel to Marx.* Cambridge: Polity Press, 1987.
Ryan, Michael. *Politics and Culture: Working Hypotheses for a Post-Revolutinary Society.* Baltimore: Johns Hopkins University Press, 1989.
Schama, Simon. *Citizens: A Chronicle of the French Revolution.* New York: Knopf, 1989.
Sennett, Richard and Cobb, Jonathan. *The Hidden Injuries of Class.* New York: Vintage, 1972.
Shils, Edward. "Daydreams and Nightmares: Reflections on the Criticism of Mass Culture." *Sewannee Review* 45 (Autumn 1957): 598.
Shumway, David. *Michel Foucault.* Boston: Twayne Publishers, 1989.
Sick, Gary. "The Election Story of the Decade." *The New York Times,* 15 April 1991, p. A17.
Singer, Peter. *Animal Liberation.* New York: Avon Books, 1975.
Sklair, Leslie. *Sociology of the Global System.* Baltimore: Johns Hopkins University Press, 1991.
Smith, Tony. *Dialectical Social Theory and Its Critics.* Albany, NY: SUNY Press, 1993.
Solomon, Robert. *In the Spirit of Hegel: A Study of G. W. F. Hegel's "Phenomonology of Spirit".* New York: Oxford University Press, 1983.
Spelman, Elizabeth Victoria. *Inessential Women: Problems of Exclusion in Feminist Thought.* Boston: Beacon Press, 1988.
Suleiman, Susan Rubin. ed. *The Female Body in Western Culture: Contemporary Perspectives.* Cambridge, MA: Harvard University Press, 1986.
Stoltenberg, John. *Refusing to be a Man: Essays on Sex and Justice.* New York: Meridian, 1989.
Tar, Zoltan. *The Frankfurt School: the Critical Theories of Max Horkheimer and Theodor W. Adorno.* New York: John Wiley, 1977.
Thompson, E. P. *The Making of the English Working Class.* New York: Vintage, 1966.
Trey, George. *Solidarity andDifference: The Politics of Enlightenment in the Aftermatrh of Modernity.* New York: SUNY, 1998.
"Textualizing the Lifeworld." presented to the RPA, Chicago, 1990.
Vaneigem, Raoul. *The Book of Pleasures.* London: Pending Press, 1983.
Volti, Rudi. *Society and Technological Change.* New York: St. Martin's Press, 1992.
Waring, Stephan. *Taylorism Transformed: Scientific Management Theory Since 1945.* Chapel Hill, NC: The University of North Carolina Press, 1991.
Weber, Max. *From Max Weber: Essays in Sociology.* Edited by H. H. Gerth and C. Wright Mills. New York: Oxford University Press, 1972.
*General Economic History.* New York: Greenberg Press, 1927.

*The Protestant Ethic and the Spirit of Capitalism.* New York: Scribner's, 1958.

*The Religion of China: Confucianism and Taoism.* Glencoe, IL: Free Press, 1951

*Theory of Social and Economic Organization.* Glencoe, IL: Free Press, 1957.

West, David. *Authenticity and Empowerment: A Theory of Liberation.* New York: Harvester Wheatsheaf, 1990.

White, Stephen K. *The Recent Work of Jürgen Habermas: Reason, Justice and Modernity.* New York: Cambridge University Press, 1988.

Wiggershaus, Rolf. *The Frankfurt School: Its History, Theories and Political Significance.* Translated by Michael Robertson. Cambridge, MA: MIT Press, 1994.

Wilkerson, William and Jeffrey Paris. *New Critical Theory: Essays on Liberation,* New York: Rowman and Littlefield, 2001.

Williams, Bernard. "The Truth in Relativism." In *Moral Luck.* Cambridge: Cambridge University Press, 1981.

Williams, Raymond. *Marxism and Literature.* Oxford: Oxford University Press, 1977.

"Towards Many Socialisms." In *Resources of Hope: Culture, Democracy, Socialism.* New York: Verso, 1989.

Winner, Langdon. *Autonomous Technology: Technics-out-of-Control as a Theme in Political Thought.* Cambridge, MA: MIT Press, 1977.

Wolin, Richard. *Labyrinths.* Amherst: University of Massachusetts Press, 1995.

Young, Iris Marion. "Polity and Group Difference: A Critique of the Ideal of Universal Citizenship." In *Feminism and political Theory.* Edited by Cass R. Sunstein. Chicago: University of Chicago Press, 1990.

"Z", "To the Stalin Mausoleum," *Deadalus* 119, (Winter 1990).

# Index

Adorno Teodor  32-45, 47, 50, 57, 58, 68, 109
Alienation  8, 9-10, 14-19, 45-46, 89
Apel, Karl Otto  62
Aronowitz, Stanley  50, 51, 53
Benhabib, Seyla  98-101
Bourdieu, Pierre  101-103
Camus, Albert  11-12
*Capital*  2-5, 10, 155n349
Class Consciousness  29, 40, 52, 92-97
Critical Theory  31-33, 40, 54, 57-62, 121n3
*Dialectic of Enlightenment*  35-40, 106
Dilthey  65, 66
*Economic and Philosophic Manuscripts of 1844*  15-20, 21, 23, 47
Feuerbach  14-17, 18, 25
Foucault  70, 91, 107, 110-114, 116
Fraser, Nancy  41, 97, 100, 107
Freud  68-72
Friere, Paulo  105
Gadamer  65-67, 105, 146n262
Habermas, Jürgen
  And the "crisis of Marxism": 56-60, 71-72
  And cognitive interests: 60-61
  On science as a social enterprise: 62-66
  And psychoanalysis: 68-70
  On the New Social Movements; 80, 86-89, 116, 117
Hegel  6-7, 9-16, 25, 28, 34, 43, 70, 78
Horkheimer, Max  32-45, 47, 57, 58
Ideal Speech Situation  74-76, 155n342

Immanent Critique  32-34
Ingram, David  87, 116
Instrumental Rationality  33, 37-40, 42-44, 46, 106
Jameson, Fredric  29, 136n156
Kant  10, 24-27, 42, 62, 74, 78
Kellner, Doug  49
*Knowledge and Human Interests*  62-66, 145n244
Kohlberg, Lawrence  79, 98-99, 153n307
*Legitimation Crisis*  74-76, 83, 93
Luhmann  78, 84-85, 153n324
Lukacs  20-30, 33-34, 46-47, 59, 79, 87
Marcuse, Herbert  40, 44-54, 68, 79, 132n106
Marx  2-8, 11, 15-20, 22-24, 56-59, 61, 68-69, 71, 78, 84, 117
McCarthy, Thomas  62, 105-106
Mead, George Herbert  9, 78, 98
*One Dimensional Man*  45-49, 52
Parsons, Talcott  9, 78, 82, 83
*Phenomenology of Spirit*  10-14
Philosophy of History  6-7, 34-35, 58
Piaget  79
Positivism  42-45, 62-63
Reification  22-24, 27-28, 34, 44
Roderick, Rick  104, 116
Rorty, Richard  118-119
Systems Theory  81-86, 105-108
*Theory of Communicative Action*  76, 78, 84, 93, 98, 104
Weber, Max  21-23, 81, 84, 113, 130n87
Young, Iris  100, 130n88, 149n284

# About The Author

J. Craig Hanks is currenty a member of the Department of Philosophy at Southwest Texas State University, after serving 9 years on the faculty of The University of Alabama in Huntsville. At SWT he serves on both the Institutional Review Board and the Institutional Animal Care and Use Committee. He has published works in Critical Theory, American Pragmatism, and in the philosophies of science, technology, and social science.